Friends, writes Peter Roebu
this book up with lots of
booze and the rest, but I ha
must be sought elsewhere;
Slices of Cricket is a collection of writings which at
once place this intelligent and talented batsman in
the front rank of cricket essayists.

The author's shrewd eye and ready wit are applied to every aspect of the game as he has experienced it. There are penetrating character studies of
his Somerset colleagues, notably Viv Richards, Ian
Botham, Sunil Gavaskar and Joel Garner; his
accounts of outstanding matches in which he took
part still make the reader catch the breath with
remembered excitement; and his more atmospheric
pieces about pre-season training, a Sunday League
game and the dressing room on a rainy day ring as
true as anything which has ever been written about
cricket from the inside.

Born in Oxford in 1956, Peter Roebuck won a scholarship to R. J. O. Mayer's Millfield School. At Cambridge he was awarded his Blue three years in succession, yet still found time to take a First in Law. In the 1975 Varsity Match at Lord's he hit 158, the second highest score by a Cambridge player in the long history of the fixture. Since his debut for Somerset he has established himself as one of the most consistent and reliable middle-order batsmen on the county circuit.

SLICES OF CRICKET

PETER ROEBUCK

London
UNWIN PAPERBACKS
Boston   Sydney

First published in Great Britain by George Allen & Unwin 1982
First published by Unwin Paperbacks 1984

UNWIN® PAPERBACKS
40 Museum Street, London WC1A 1LU, UK

Unwin Paperbacks
Park Lane, Hemel Hempstead, Herts HP2 4TE, UK

George Allen & Unwin Australia Pty Ltd
8 Napier Street, North Sydney, NSW 2060, Australia

British Library Cataloguing in Publication Data

Roebuck, Peter, *1956–*
    Slices of cricket.
1. Cricket
I. Title
796.35′8′0924   GV917
ISBN 0–04–796088–4

Set in 10 on 12 point Plantin by Nene Phototypesetters Ltd, Northampton
and printed in Great Britain
by Hazell Watson and Viney Limited,
Member of the BPCC Group,
Aylesbury, Bucks

As this could be the only book I write, I'd better dedicate it to all my friends and family. Namely . . .

My parents
My relations
Vic and Anna
Sara
Nigel, Ingy and Buckles
Pete and Eeva (thanks for the typing!)
Viv
Roy and Lynn
Ian
Joel
RJO
Norman Teer
Everyone in Greece
Everyone in Australia
And everyone I've forgotten.

Contents

Illustrations

Preface

'I was so pleased to see that *Slices of Cricket* received such a favourable review in Somerset handbook, and I wasn't surprised to learn that you had written it yourself'.

So wrote Vic Marks in a letter to me a couple of winters ago. I'm afraid I must reveal the truth. If you scour the 1982 Somerset handbook you will find a most kind review of this book. It says among other things that 'this is a book full of good humour and variety . . . . I particularly cherish his hilarious piece on Norman Teer . . . . it's a lively book essential for all Somerset cricket followers'.

Well I wrote that! I may never be a famous author but I will be, I suspect, one of the very few to write his own first review!

I wrote this book between June 1979 and September 1981. Most of the pieces are ageless, only the articles on Botham and Richards are out of date. *Ian Botham* was written during 1981 when his fortunes were at their lowest ebb. Typically he bounced back a few months later to turn on its head a thrilling Ashes series. He has returned as England's leading cricketer, a man to dominate his age. My views on Ian have changed too. Were I to write this article now I would place less emphasis on his gung-ho, daredevil spirit and more on his ambitions. Ian reminds me a bit of Macbeth; a heroic figure, a fine stirring warrior, and a man plagued by ambition to lead his nation. He remains a cricketer of immense courage, a man of considerable force.

As for the piece on Viv I regret that I was not more personal. Viv is an emotional cauldron, anyone who is not a little afraid of him does not know him. He is also a kind, considerate man who cares a great deal about those he regards as friends. When I was in my deepest depression, as failure heaped upon failure, it was Viv who sorted me out and lent the support of his formidable personality. He is cricket's toughest character, and yet his strength is often missed hidden as it is behind the politeness and humility he learned to value as a youngster.

Let me leave you with a couple of foot notes. Norman Teer rang me after this book was published to pass on another story (see Chapter 13). Apparently he had brought himself on to bowl with two runs needed for victory and the last pair in. He served up a juicy long hop outside leg stump. The delighted batsman swung at the ball, cracked it a little late and succeeded only in hitting the ball into the keeper's belly. As the keeper fell the ball nestled into his stomach to bring another victory!

And another side of Viv Richards (Chapter 4). I was batting with him against Surrey at Weston Super Mare and he was blazing the ball all round the ground. He was particularly severe on leg spinner Intikhab Alam who was bowling very well, still going for at least ten every over. Before another Intikhab over Viv sauntered down the pitch in his deceptively laxadasical way to enquire how I thought 'Inti' was bowling. 'Very well' I replied. Viv nodded, pottered back to his crease and proceeded to block the next six balls with immaculate forward defensives, just to give Intikhab a maiden to cheer him up a bit!

Slices of Cricket

1

A New Season

As the old song says, 'Mad dogs and Englishmen go out in the midday sun'. I doubt if rabies is strong enough a disease to persuade a demented dog to venture out into the cold winds and gusty showers to play cricket today. But then it is 1 April (appropriately enough) and a new season has begun. Our overseas stars will not return for a few weeks yet, they're playing Test cricket in some sun-drenched corner of the world. They'll appear, shivering and pale, towards the end of the month in time to play the first game. They need less practice than the rest of us, because they are better and anyhow bat and bowl all the year round. So it's we English professionals alone who must suffer the worst of April. Biting easterlies sweep layers of sweaters aside, cutting through to send damp chills down spines. In an early-season game at Oxford once we fielded in five sweaters and as many of Derek Taylor's long johns as we could muster and still froze. It's not so easy to catch in the slips with blue fingers.

And the irony of it is, we've been looking forward to this all winter.

Anyhow, as we assemble at the County Ground, so depressed and decrepit in winter, it begins to throb with the life of spring. Officials, groundsmen and secretaries are pleased to see us: they've toiled throughout the dark months without thanks and can at least see the reason for it all now.

Cricketers drive in through Jack White's old gates. A hard man, Jack, they say. A left-arm spinner of uncanny accuracy and cantankerous temperament, he bowled with outstanding economy, disturbing the received opinion that cricket in those days was full of dash and sparkle. I expect there were quite a few dour old pros, too.

Everyone hails everyone with immense gusto. Cries of 'What, are you still on the staff?' and 'Who's captain this year, then?' are gradually replaced by 'What about Hoddle's effort the other day?'

or 'I'd shoot those beggars in Ireland'. Politically most Somerset cricketers stand to the right of Mrs Thatcher, though few of them have much interest in politics. Dennis Breakwell and Jeremy Lloyds are much more likely to be able to list the heroes of *The Great Escape* than to name the President of France.

Naturally, this burst of cheeriness will not survive the month. There are bound to be a few rows to liven things up a bit. Our captain and his aides must apply rules with discretion or we'd all be suspended indefinitely! Rules applicable to soccer players cannot be forced on cricketers. You can instruct your inside-left to be asleep by 10 pm every night; far more difficult to persuade your no. 3 to have an early night before a match day. Every day is a match day, and maybe no. 3 enjoys a night out from time to time. Several Somerset players do not find their beds before midnight, and one or two sleep much later. One was out until 3 am the night before our victory in the 1979 Gillette Cup Final. With pressure every day, and steadily mounting during the season, cricketers develop robust constitutions able to withstand tension during the day and gin during the night.

Still we must train together in April, and we might as well start as mates. We change into a variety of tracksuits, to risk the frosty morning air. Not all of the giants of the past would have appreciated this much. Graham Burgess would not have enjoyed the strenuous muscle-stretching we do every day. If he'd wanted to do that sort of thing he'd have chosen to play rugby or soccer. Traditionally cricket has been a less physical game, has required mental agility more than gymnastic flexibility. But as limited-over cricket strengthens its grip, so the ageing and the rotund hang up their boots earlier.

Our tracksuits have shrunk alarmingly during the winter. Obviously that new, blue washing powder shrinks everything it touches. Several players make mental notes not to use it on their underwear. Eventually, though, we trot out into the fresh, supposedly invigorating air of April. Mist grips each breath and a bleak greyness dominates the skies. Peter Robinson, our coach, suggests that we warm up by jogging round the boundary. This we do, at our own cumbersome pace, amidst considerable puffing and panting. Then a few exercises. It is soon evident that our Peter has passed a jolly winter, Scrooge-like, poring over books to discover new muscles and devising new ways of twanging them. Our hamstrings sound like duelling banjos, and agonised yelps mix with the blue words that litter every conversation.

Peter is only temporarily in charge, though. Soon our Australian physio, Dennis Waight, will return. Since Dennis spends a fair bit of his time calling Joel Garner 'a big tart', or running ten miles followed by a 2½-mile swim, you will gather that he is a hard man. He 'bites yer legs', as they say.

We try to touch the ground with the palms of our hands and with straight legs. Palms of hands! Good grief, man, I can barely touch the tops of the blades of grass. Possibly my legs have grown an inch or two, maybe some damn' fool cut the grass yesterday. Not all of us struggle. Hallam Moseley, a lithe, black fast bowler, finds the task ridiculously easy. Peter Denning, on the other hand, just about reaches his shins. But then, he's had his benefit.

It's so damnably cold, and anyway will all this help me to get off the mark at Oxford on 29 April?

Sweat spreads as shuttle runs and sprints heap upon each other. These sessions will be harder by next week, and we'll start the season as fit as most professional sportsmen. Not that we want to be quite at our peak. It's a long season and it's no bad idea (especially for bowlers) to begin the season, as horses do, carrying a pound or two. It'll soon vanish when things get going.

A young professional is dispatched to brew the tea. We all did these little chores in our apprentice years – I worked the scoreboard, even helped build stands. Shrewdly he makes the tea none too well; he'll not be appointed tea-lady again. Comments question its quality, and the intelligence of the youngster. He'll find it worse as twelfth man. I remember, at Hove, running the after-match communal bath and omitting to keep an eye on it. As Somerset trooped wearily from the field I rushed into the changing room, suddenly aware of 'the great thing of me forgot'. I discovered the appalling sight of water gushing over the brim of the bath. I jumped in, whites and all, to pull out the plug. I grabbed a brush and swished away the water. Just as my team ascended the steps I jumped into the bath to replace the plug. Then I hurriedly removed my wet whites and awaited my colleagues' entrance. No-one noticed my pale face or sweating brow.

After our cuppa we shower and head for the Ring Of Bells for lunch. Without being quite as insouciant these days, cricketers can still sip a pint or two. A nip of brandy before batting is not so common now but gin and tonics still flow freely. Of course gin is the drink of the swashbuckler, the musketeer, the man of adventure and style. At Cambridge an erstwhile team-mate danced elegantly down the pitch at 6.25 pm to essay a flourishing drive. We all joined him a few minutes later, and I followed him to the bar with grave suspicions. He duly ordered, in splendid tones, a large gin and tonic. He did not play again.

Sad to say I manage only half of bitter to accompany my ploughman's. Then back to the ground for a Company meeting. Our Führer (as Brian Rose is somewhat charitably dubbed) runs our cricket and business affairs. Few of us feel at home with a brief-case and I know of only one cricketer who buys the *Financial Times*. So Brian Rose negotiates, runs our Company and handles financial affairs. As for the cricket, he says we must all pull together. I suppose he could not very well suggest that we fight tooth and nail, spitting at each other in corridors. But cricket teams rarely resemble the Magnificent Seven in unity, not with a dozen renegades vying for the available horses.

After our meeting we change into hastily dug-up whites. Surprisingly, this does not cause an immediate downpour. We must not use the indoor school because of the Flower Show (England, this England!), so we inspect the grass pitches. Batsmen push and poke, shaking their heads doubtfully, declaring that 'they're a bit green'. Meanwhile the bowlers express the view that the wickets are as flat as pancakes, and that any batsman worth his salt 'could score runs on them with a stick of rhubarb'. This difference of opinion will accompany every inspection before every game.

The nets are serious, but not as tense as matches. Batsmen hit in the air, attempt drives on the up and dance smoothly down the pitch. Might as well make hay now, we'll mostly be grim by May. Spin-bowlers suffer most: Dennis Breakwell, disappearing over the hoardings for the umpteenth time, glares at the batsman as if to say, 'Why don't you do that in matches, then?' Peter Robinson loses a ball or two in the Tone, though not as many as he will when Ian Botham returns. Ian likes to whack as many balls as possible into the river, provoking outrage dismissed with guffaws.

Cricketers are different in nets. Strangely, fast bowlers are yards quicker. Yet the strip is the self-same 22 yards in length. David Gurr, who left cricket for insurance, bowls superbly in nets still, with pace and movement. Hard to realise that at Bristol in 1978 David delivered seven wides in his first over, several others being ignored by a kind umpire. He tried to complete the over by simply turning his arm over from a one-pace run. The ball came straight to me at third slip. A terrifying psychological difference persists when the net is removed.

After nets, we field. It's too cold to catch cricket balls, too bitter to stretch muscles by throwing. We are an excellent fielding team: where else could you find four fast bowlers who field as brilliantly as Garner, Dredge, Moseley and Botham?

Finally, our work is done for the day. We soak in the communal bath, catching up with the scandal. Who has left whom? Who has one in the oven again? Gossip thrives. Then we depart through the Jack Whites. Our cars range from glossy and sponsored to rattling bangers. Strange how it's the Varsity boys ('the professors') who drive the latter.

2

Ian Botham

Once every year Ian Botham repairs to Scotland. He descends upon Callandar, a village hidden in the remote mountains north of Stirling, for all the world like Bonnie Prince Charlie returned to claim his rightful title. Ostensibly Botham arrives for a holiday, a rest from his strenuous lifestyle. The Scots, a hardy, resolute race, spend the 51 weeks between Ian's visits recovering their strength, preparing their stamina for next April. Not the Gathering of the Clans, nor the Butcher of Culloden, caused as many sore heads and reeling stomachs as a week with Botham.

Each day Ian rises with the McLarks, eats a hearty breakfast and walks to the river to stand waist-deep in freezing water for 12 hours holding a stick with a piece of string attached. His hope is to land a salmon, the king of the rivers. A corps of reporters and photographers accompany Ian, to capture the historic day when a salmon is hauled proudly ashore. They've waited for four fruitless (fishless?) years, despite efforts to persuade an insulted Botham to buy a salmon at the nearest fishmonger and to be photographed with it. Ian stays through the howling winds and lashing rain, stock still in the water for hours on end. His attendant crew are not quite so dedicated and organise a rota system lest they all collapse with pneumonia.

Each night Ian repairs entirely content, fish or no fish, to the local hostelry. It is in this snug corner that Ian exhausts his hosts by sampling every variety of whisky stocked and, what's more, demanding that everyone around keeps pace, man for man, drink for drink. There are 135 different scotches in the pub and Ian is only in for six nights so the pace is hectic. One by one his friends shrink away, bowed and beaten. Botham beds in the early hours of the morning to rise again a few hours later, full of beans, to repeat the dose. It rarely takes anything more than a pork pie to refresh Ian.

Even the journalists, not a notoriously sober crew, fall by the wayside, unable to survive life at such a crack. And this is the annual holiday! The image in Scotland of the genteel Englishman at his ease, nibbling cucumber sandwiches and sipping tea, lies in ruins. In Scotland Botham is in his element, a Monarch of the Glen to satisfy Compton Mackenzie. Should the clans rise Botham will be there, swinging his club, clobbering to the right and to the left. No doubt he could toss a mere caber, and he could fling decorous ladies around the room at the ceilidh with the best of them.

This is Ian Botham enjoying life. Whether hunting, shooting, fishing, kicking, bowling or drinking, he resembles a baron of those wild mediaeval days. He drives his car, as they rode their horses, with panache. His instincts are not tamed, his zest for life has not mellowed. His whole-heartedness leads to triumphs and troubles, to success and scrapes, for it is not balanced by a shrewd appreciation of public relations nor by a tolerance of rudeness or criticism. At Hove last year I rebuked him for his hostility towards an autograph-hunter in a bar. He replied, angrily, that if I received the threatening, nasty letters he did I'd be wary of casual admirers, too.

Ian and I spend a fair bit of time chatting together, the supposedly studious intellectual and the supposedly arrogant sportsman. We've known each other for 14 years, ever since we played for Somerset's Under-15 team. Already he was a brash, daring youngster willing to have a go at various activities attempted by most of us rather later in life. As a cricketer, though, he gave few signs of unusual talent. Despite occasional spectacular contributions, he did not reach the England Schoolboys team – Slocombe, Marks and Roebuck did. He was indignant, still is, reminding me that we once put on 95 of which he scored 83. And I was picked! Personally I'm not convinced of the accuracy of this story. Surely I must have scored 15 at least?

We were all delighted when he packed his bags and joined the Lord's ground staff. At least we might enjoy some peace. At Lord's he was, as ever, quickly the life and soul of things. Inevitably he suffered his initiation whitewashing several times, for the young man needed discipline, but it was not long before he was in charge of the whitewashing squad. He lived with Rodney Ontong in a small flat, where they made no effort whatsoever to live within their means. They decided that they could not possibly spread their wages far enough, and preferred one good binge to blow it all away. After that they cajoled and persuaded funds from friends. Ian was not a great worrier in those days; tomorrow would look after itself.

After two years learning his trade at Lord's, Botham joined Somerset. 1974 was a good vintage at Taunton, bringing Richards, Marks, Roebuck and Slocombe too. With his strength and aggression, Ian was the first of the young Englishmen to play. His debut was against Lancashire, a contest which confused spectators since Roebuck and Marks were running the scoreboard. Botham announced himself by cracking three fierce boundaries before tamely offering a catch to short extra cover. He returned to the pavilion in a cloud of dust, storming into the dressing room to utter the oft-repeated words, 'I should have belted the ruddy thing harder.' Most of us, upon being caught, regret having hit the ball in the air at all. Already Botham's only sorrow lay in not having hit it higher.

Even in those early games Ian was not exactly a blushing maiden. From the very start he was fiercely competitive, determined to take the game to the opposition. His explosive exchanges, mostly on the field, with Brian Close brightened things up at Taunton. Once Ian stopped a ball brilliantly, surprising the batsmen who found themselves at the same end. Instead of trotting to the stumps to flick off a bail, Ian hurled the ball at the wickets, demolishing them. Close was furious, and rightly so, for the risk was foolish. There was much arm-waving and gesticulating before things simmered down. Two similar characters, Close and Botham, and their regard for each other grew with each row.

That Ian hit the stumps was typical; his luck guarded him through many difficulties, and it held a long time. Four years later he joined in a Melbourne Cup draw with his 17 touring colleagues. They had two horses each. Ian's came in first and second. No-one was surprised.

But fortune is selective, it favours the bold adventurer. If Ian was lucky, he deserved to be. He took heroic liberties, not all of them calculated with minute care. He accepted challenges for the hell of it, for the fun of it. When I played against him at Fenner's I waited until he had settled in his stance for his first ball, then I asked my deep mid-wicket to advance ten yards in from the boundary. Ian's eyes lit up and notions of playing himself in were immediately scrapped – my invitation to clear the fielder could not be resisted. He swung massively, mis-hit and the ball drifted just over my man to bounce inside the ropes for a four. He guffawed, finding the whole thing hilarious. He would have laughed if the teasing had succeeded.

Another example. At Oxford, Somerset had narrowly failed in a run chase. We needed 17 off the last ball. Botham went for them – and was caught at long-off! He could be outrageous, but it did not worry him. He never doubted his destiny.

Of course luck was not his only quality. He is outstandingly courageous, too. Early in his career he was struck on the temple by an Andy Roberts bouncer but carried on to guide his team to victory, with the improbable support of Hallam, Moseley and Bob Clapp. Nor has he been known to flinch in the face of the battery of West Indian fast bowlers, though even he tires of the constant barrage.

With his luck and his fortitude Botham bestrode the cricket scene, a Roy of the Rovers. He batted majestically, fielded brilliantly and bowled incisively. His bowling, perhaps, showed the attraction of the man, all burly determination and bold variation. His run-up was not smooth, nor was his delivery stride consistent, but his striking rate was high. He bowled teams out at all levels, never caring much how. He was, and is, no purist: he derives every bit as much pleasure from trapping a batsman with a wild delivery as in trimming his bails with a perfect outswinger. Once he induced Warwickshire batsmen to hook his bouncer to long leg – Jameson, Kanhai and Kallicharran included – and did not bat an eyelid in surprise.

Ian unsettled batsmen. They never knew what on earth the youngster might do next. And with a run-up full of bounce, an action full of nip and an eye wicked with defiance, he was an unpredictable handful. Even in his first year as an England player Botham retained this wild, optimistic, vigorous approach. If he was failing he looked absurdly out of his depth, a young man raised before his time. His first Test spell, against Greg Chappell's tourists, was expensive. They made easy meat of his inaccurate away-swingers. Brearley did not bring him back until mid-afternoon, not wanting to lose his grip on the match. Botham's loosener somehow or other induced Chappell to play on. Chappell was distraught to have fallen to so unworthy a delivery. Botham seized the moment, rode his luck and finished with five wickets. Critics said it was a fluke, but quickly realised that flukes do not repeat themselves so often.

After that breakthrough Ian strode from success to success, dominating international cricket. Against teams weakened by the World Series rival Botham broke record upon record. He worked hard, too, improving his technique. Mike Hendrick in particular helped him to develop a smooth run-up. These days Ian very rarely bowls a no-ball: his feet land in precisely the same well-worn tracks every time.

This same Botham, in the Indian Golden Jubilee Test match, bowled wellnigh 50 overs, took 13 wickets and rescued his side from 58 for 5 with a mighty 114. He effectively carried his travel-weary, depressed team on his broad shoulders. And, I dare say, during that remarkable, responsible innings, he risked much, sweeping Doshi from outside off stump or cutting from a length as his impulses took him. But his luck held, and praise followed.

It seemed as if Ian's golden youth would never end. Yet quite suddenly it did. In 1980 he experienced sustained failure for the first time in his life and it did not rain, it poured.

Suddenly he was under attack from all quarters. Newspapers said he was overweight. They stooped so low as to ask Liam (his four-year-old son) to describe Papa's eating habits. He was prevented from playing soccer for Scunthorpe. His name hit the headlines for speeding and assault charges. As England's new captain he was heavily criticised for his lack of form and worst of all in Trinidad in 1981 for his 'irresponsible' swipe at Viv Richards' gentle off-break. Suddenly Ian's every move was subject to close scrutiny and intense analysis. Where before his indiscretions had been tolerated as a part of his Viking spirit, now his failures were held up and scorned. Ian did not thrive in this vexed limelight. Frustrated by his inability to defy single-handedly the fierce West Indian pace attack, his cricket became self-conscious. The vitriolic critics of his poor shot against Richards closed his personality up, prevented him playing his natural, vigorous game. His Test performances sank, newspaper men feared his flame had been extinguished and certainly much of his fire, much of the bubbling confidence, was missing. His cricket was inhibited and his personality too tense to relax. As captain of England he resembled a caged tiger.

Eventually the wheel came full circle, to everyone's delight. Botham resigned as England's captain, aware that his reign was over anyhow. Suddenly he blossomed again, winning three Test matches and the Ashes for England by a series of devastating performances. His batting was more mighty, more majestic than it had ever been before. His bowling recovered much of its wit and sparkle and, at last, he was catching flies in the slips again.

No doubt Brearley did much to stimulate this revival, encouraging Ian to open out his personality, to have the courage to risk all again. Perhaps Brearley might have, when Botham holed out off Richards that infamous time, rebuked Ian for not hitting out but for holding back, just as Ian himself had done in his first county game.

For Ian has not changed. If anything, he has calmed down a bit! His pranks are fewer, though they are much more widely publicised. He is still brash and aggressive, still a generous friend who stoops to foolishness only to thwart your anger with a guffaw. He is well-liked by cricketers who know him. In 1980, for all his troubles, he managed to bat at a benefit game in absolutely torrential rain. He scored 85. Next day it was too wet even for Botham, so he went out to kick a football about to entertain the crowd. He later hired a helicopter to fly down to Glastonbury to appear in a benefit soccer match – at his own expense. He contributes generously, though privately, to charities, and keeps us all alive and cheerful with his gin and tonics and his guffaws. Oh, yes, and even in his troubled year of 1980, he did top our batting averages.

3

A Run Chase

A gentle game, cricket. It attracts gentlemen, scholars, vicars, cobblers, mild men of many hues. Not too much strain or stress, a pleasant afternoon in green pastures, basking in the warm rays of the sun. A time of ease, a time to unwind from the cares of life. A time for reflection, a time to recite the poems of one's youth, a time to revel in the pleasing sound of leather on helmet.

And then the other team's innings closes. A rude awakening. We're chasing 209 in 40 overs. Get out the fags, strap on the pads, bite the nails, it's going to be a wild, wild run-chase.

Oh, it's all right for the bowlers. They collapse into a chair, remove boots and dubious socks and sink into a bath to restore life to weary limbs. It's the batsmen who must rush out to bat, sweat still dripping from their hairy chests.

Out go the openers. 'Must get off to a solid start,' says the captain, 'but don't fall behind the clock.' 'Score eight an over, don't slog and don't get out,' translates the coach. Everyone wanders up into the 'box', a cubicle from which the players view the game. Several have pads on, more than usual in fact. Our captain has decided that he'll go in if the left-arm spinner comes on, whilst you're to go in if the nasty fast bowler stays on.

Off to a quiet start. No-one says anything. 28 for 0 in nine overs. A bit slow, but no men lost. Our skipper is on his third small cigar already, our wicket-keeper is reading his second 'lively' magazine – he says that he hates 'em, but that he's checking 'em out for the junior pro's. No. 4 has visited the gents twice already. Others are reading papers or solving crosswords, but all with one eye on the cricket.

The crowd is restless: 46 for 0 in 14 overs, mainly in scampered singles. Our rivals are fielding well, denying us every run with miserly dives. Shouts of 'C'mon, Dapper' and 'Get a move on, Nipper' escape from supporters. Even in the box people are edgy, nervous. Comments on the game add to the slightly depressed atmosphere. Umpires are criticised. 'That's a wide,' says our senior pro, and a wide is signalled. 'Well I'm blowed,' he says. 'Long two in that,' calls no. 4, as if anyone on the field could hear.

Finally a wicket falls, 'Nipper' superbly caught at point. Strangely this lightens the mood, something has broken at least, the phoney war is over.

No. 3 enters to the cheers of the crowd. He's our best player, hero of many a noble hour. He'll soon sort things out, the crowd reckon. First ball he flashes wildly; groans rumble around the ground and fielders raise their hands to the skies, hoping. He's on tenterhooks, determined to attack from the start. 'What sort of a shot was that?' exclaims our senior pro. Our wicket-keeper sighs and reaches for another magazine, whilst his captain refrains from comment – he must maintain an air of cool, detached confidence even if his hair is rapidly greying.

69 for 1 in 18 overs. We need 140 in 22 overs. Difficult, but those nine wickets will be handy. Lancashire, in their Gillette Cup triumphs of the early 1970s, were often well behind the clock but always with their best wickets intact.

A couple of successful overs follow. 'Dapper' is holding firm, scurrying a few singles, and no. 3 is cutting loose. The field is retreating, things are alive, more men on the boundary now.

Disaster! Dapper calls for a sharp single, no. 3 is slow out of the blocks. 'Hurry up,' says Dapper as they cross. That's never a good sign – not quite as bad as 'sorry' though! Accurate throw, 'keeper whips off the bails. 'Out,' decides the umpire. No. 3 traipses disconsolately back to the pavilion. Silence in the box, cigarettes lit, as the atmosphere thickens with smoke and tension.

No. 4 joins Dapper at the crease, his nerves vanishing as he becomes involved in the game. 86 for 2 in 21 overs: tight, very tight.

The crowd is on tenterhooks, edgy, twitching like a crab in its death throes. To win the League, Somerset must win its easy games easily, close finishes must be few and far between for some are bound to slip away.

A running commentary from the pavilion. 'Well bowled', 'Bite, ball, bite', 'German General' (this an encouragement for the ball to race to the boundary, as is 'Goeballs'), 'Wide', 'Hit the thing, man'. The box mysteriously fills with reserves, committee, friends. All study the game with intense concentration – no crossword puzzles now.

We still have some dangerous batsmen in hand, but we'll have to bat very well to win. Still, these 40-over games can swing remarkably quickly.

Leather begins to fly. Each ball brings some new incident. Explosive events heap upon each other. Wickets, boundaries, leg-byes, overthrows, yahoos, wild swishes, nudges, pokes and prods in desperate succession. Groans, sighs, cheers, stunned silence, restlessness.

184 for 6 in 36 overs. Another 'diarrhoea finish'! Dennis Breakwell and 'Pops' Popplewell are in now. They run well together these two, nodding, winking, scampering.

Oh, no! A ludicrous run, trying to push a single to the 'keeper. 'Out if he hits,' laments our senior pro; and he hits!

190 for 7 in 37 overs. No. 11 is padding up. He wears spectacles, still can't see the ball, and went in at no. 11 when he could! Not a reassuring prospect. 19 wanted in three overs. The field is widespread, lots of singles available. But the fast bowlers are on now, and our weakest batsmen are in. Brian Close maintained that you should chase a target imagining you have one less over than you have, a bit like having a few trumps in reserve if things suddenly go drastically wrong. No chance of that this time – we'll need every last ball.

Predictions and comments run thick and fast in the packed box. Cigarettes are puffed, sentences left unfinished as a hush descends for every delivery. Dennis is out, 201 for 8. One over left, eight runs to win: real boys' comic stuff, terrific.

Two singles snatched off the first two balls. A flash at the third ball fails to connect. Real dire straits! Six in three balls. Next ball is slashed and flies off the edge of the bat to the unpatrolled fine third-man boundary. The captain's nightmare, these edges: they rush so quickly to the ropes.

Two in two balls. Surely it's in the bag now? Yet last time we were in this position we lost. Our bespectacled no. 11 tried two violent swipes and missed both! Not a happy day.

The fieldsmen close in. Colin Dredge pushes forward, a single is scampered. A leg-bye. But wait a minute! Bedlam! Colin is out lbw! The umpire is called all the names under the Australian sun in the box, until Colin reports that 'it must have been close' – the nearest most men get to agreeing with an umpire's verdict.

It's all on our no. 11 of dubious reputation. We guide him towards the stumps. 'Seymour' we call him, as he resembles in appearance and flourish that noble West Indian batsman, Seymour Nurse.

The bowler sends down his fastest delivery, straining for extra pace. 'Seymour' does not swipe, he caresses the ball as Casanova caressed Josephine (or was it Hardy?). It races off his bat and flashes past point to the third-man boundary. The game is over, the match won. 'Never in doubt,' whispers our senior pro, as might Private Fraser of *Dad's Army* fame. 10,000 supporters cheer. Our players collapse in chairs, even those who have not been playing. Whoops of joy subside into exhausted smiles.

Roll on a pleasant, dignified three-day game tomorrow. We live like vicars: Monday to Saturday pass in amiable tranquillity, visiting maiden aunts or bowling maiden overs, before the onslaught continues on Sunday. I wonder whether vicars or Sunday League cricketers pray hardest on the Sabbath?

4

Viv

Le style, c'est l'homme, as whatsisname put it, whilst sipping champagne from a lady's boot. So it is with batsmen. He who strokes the ball with loving care is a gentleman. He who studies it with hawk eyes is a worried man. He who blocks fast bowlers and belts spinners is a wise man.

Isaac Vivian Alexander Richards (the amiable 'Viv' is left in the dressing room) has the style of a champion. He is as erect as a proud man should be, and as fierce as Smokin' Joe Frazier. He wears no helmet, nor any other extra padding. He does not need it, will not give the merest hint to the bowler of fear or fallibility. And so he stands there, an intimidating, daunting man on the field, immensely polite and friendly off it.

Viv was brought up in a hard school. Facing Anderson Roberts as a boy with little padding on a pitch less reliable than Iago toughens the resolve. Survival produced a competitive, courageous cricketer. For Viv supports his prodigious ability with resource and courage. His response to being hit on the temple by a Hogg bumper was to dispatch the next ball into the twelfth row at square leg. At times Viv provokes fast bowlers to do their damnedest. Facing Len Pascoe in Sydney, he hooked a mighty boundary and replied to Pascoe's lethal glare by a teasing 'Butter, Lennie, butter'. Next ball a vicious bouncer was cracked for six and Pascoe's comments were cut short by Richards' 'Marmalade, Lennie, marmalade'! You need to be very good, and very brave, to provoke a man as strong as Pascoe. And all the while Viv smiled a gentle smile.

'Smokey' bats with the passionate intensity of a murderer rather than the cool rationality of an assassin. If he is steamed up, as he sometimes is in big games or against particular bowlers, he bats with the mean aggression of Tommy Hearns or Marvin Hagler. His face becomes almost contorted by the intensity of his effort on these occasions, much as Brian Close's used to when he breathed defiance. Viv does not always attain this fierce majesty, but when he does he bats with fury. In Yorkshire, provoked by a rude and raucous crowd, he tore into the bowling, wanting only to explode his anger by 'beating the ball'. And in a Gillette Cup game against Warwickshire in 1978 he applied himself with every ounce of his deep fund of energy and scored 135. On both occasions he survived confident appeals for catches behind the wicket: Viv always walks, but not when steamed up.

That is Richards at his greatest, utterly determined to destroy the attack. More often, certainly in county games, he bats in relaxed vein, as if he has no mission to accomplish, no opponent to demolish. His love of boxing finds expression in his batting, with its lethal, short blows, only in heated, edgy games. On less vital days he smiles, appears sleepy and gently teases friends and foe alike. On those days he may tear into bowlers but he does not break their hearts. There is no sense of inevitability in Richards' innings in his lighter moods. Hope springs eternal.

Not that his technique has escaped criticism. Anguished bowlers for long held to the belief that Viv swung across the line of the ball too often to last. Upon his arrival in London for a trial, Alf Gover advised him to use more top hand and left shoulder, saying that he'd never succeed in England's damp, unreliable conditions unless he played straight. For a few months Viv respected these strictures, arriving at Taunton as a powerful back-foot player who could square drive past point at will. He showed no signs of a leg-side bias. Those sizzling drives through mid-wicket became dominant a year later, as Richards emerged as a Test star.

Of course Richards can bat with skill and even technical perfection if he so desires. Some of his innings for Somerset on awkward wickets have been as masterful as any back-to-the-wall effort by Boycott. He scored 89, years ago, against Sussex on a raging turner, a wicket on which most of us struggled to survive for a few minutes. He defended his wicket with prodigiously careful forward defensives; so careful were they that everyone on the ground supposed that Richards was teasing the bowler. And, in a way, he was. It was one demonstration, and there have been many others, of technical mastery to convince the harshest critic. Alf Gover would have been delighted. Yet Richards was teasing. He'd decided to display his defensive skills but he could have cut loose at any moment. He is so good that he does not need to defend on bad wickets. That is why he only plays long defensive innings if he is in a particularly impish mood.

In any case, those mid-wicket drives from off stump are not as hazardous as they appear. For a very long time the bat comes through the line of the ball; only at the last minute do steely wrists deflect its trajectory to find some yawning gap through the leg-side. Nevertheless bowlers for a season or two glared ferociously as respectable off-stump deliveries disappeared to the ropes at mid-wicket. Arms were raised, heads shaken, knowing glances exchanged between wizened professionals. But Viv hardly ever missed that shot, so that nowadays even accurate away-swing bowlers are reluctant to aim at off stump – or anywhere within reach! Last season Jim Cumbes did offer one ball on the stumps. It started on middle, swung late towards the slips and was duly dispatched with utter certainty to the mid-wicket boundary. 'Never again,' sighed the saddened bowler.

Richards does look fallible: there's just a chance he might decide to hit the next ball over extra cover, or maybe he'll charge down the wicket with nothing particular in mind. He's even been caught hooking first ball off that most idiosyncratic of bowlers, Mushtaq Mohammad. And on a quiet day you stand a fair chance of running him out (or more likely, his partner). Batsmen as aristocratic in their splendour as IVA do not always quite understand that, while he feasts on boundaries, others must scavenge singles.

Weaknesses are less evident these days as Richards' powers of concentration match the intensity of his effort. Of course, so strong a determination to win has its hazards. Failure becomes all the more difficult to accept. Although Viv rarely displays disappointment to opponent or spectator, those privileged enough to share a dressing room with him witness the disgust at failure, or the infrequent explosions as the cauldron boils over. Various broken windows around the world, a few blind umpires and several ignorant spectators can testify that Smokey does not always accept the slings and arrows of fortune with much enthusiasm. Viv's standards are high, for himself and for others, and do not encourage the glad sufferance of fools nor the ready acceptance of defeat. Soon, though, the smile returns and with it the zest for life that chases the near past into more remote parts of the memory.

It is only in his batting that Richards reaches (on occasions) this crescendo of effort. He plays the rest of his cricket with a slightly mischievous air, with a twinkle never far from his eye. Smokey bowls in several styles. He has stolen Test wickets with his off-breaks, has bowled medium pace accurately in one-day games and has even resorted to a mixture of leg-breaks, googlies, bouncers, off-breaks and top-spinners (and that's just the first over!) if proceedings are in need of a little sparkle. In this last style Richards has worried not a few batsmen, and rather more fielders.

But for all the limitations of his bowling, it is often to Viv that teams turn in times of trouble. His personal stature, his determination to win and his joy in being a part of a team help to add spice and menace to apparently harmless deliveries. He bowled his overs uncomplainingly in the 1979 World Cup final, even finding sufficient courage to glare at Clive Lloyd when he dropped Geoffrey Boycott. That Richards greatly admired Lloyd's leadership was irrelevant. He builds himself up to perform at the highest possible level on the big occasions and demands that everyone else should do the same. His determination inspires colleagues, though it might disturb those of meek temperament, and his team-mates well understand that his bursts of anger are only expressions of his irresistible will to win. In fact they are delighted that he still has this enthusiasm after his years at the top.

As a fielder, Viv is brilliant anywhere. If things have been a little hectic the night before he may be spotted at slip, otherwise he lurks in the gully or prowls in the outfield. He enjoys tempting providence if the game is dull. He'll catch skyscrapers with a nonchalance they do not always deserve. Sometimes even Viv comes unstuck. Once he tried to catch a batsman behind his back, this ploy having brought the house down in a benefit game. Alas, the timing was awry and the catch spilt. The bowler's comments were not recorded. Often batsmen are invited to test the power of his throw. Few accept these invitations (as one would be reluctant to respond to a luncheon appointment with Lucrezia Borgia). Occasionally some brave soul takes his chance. During a Sunday League game at Lord's, Richards fielded a ball on the far distant Tavern boundary and stood still, indicating that the batsmen might, if they saw fit, run a second. Mike Gatting rose to the challenge, heroically advanced five yards down the wicket, was sent back and didn't make it.

Such displays of unbridled confidence make IVA a stimulating colleague, respected by cricketers. His centuries in the World, Gillette and Benson and Hedges Cup finals surprised no-one who knew him. None of the innings was remarkable for spectacular hitting or brilliant strokeplay. They were controlled and conclusive assertions of Richards' stature. And his performances in Australia, especially the extraordinary 154 in Melbourne in 1979, underlined this supremacy while hinting that the King nowadays needs some extra spice in the match if he is to perform at his best.

The unrelenting succession of big matches puts a tremendous strain even on so balanced an individual as I. V. A. Richards. Inevitably he cannot always be on top form. To survive he needs to relax and enjoy himself as much as possible. Viv's favourite outlet is the golf course, where he can belt away without inhibition and let off steam without offence. It is well documented that only those with a notion of the futility of things can safely play golf. Rational behaviour has no place on the links (or at the wheel of a car). For how can a man be reasonable when the fates are so perverse? Golf is a provoking game. To be able to hit a ball travelling fast at one's head for a massive six, yet to watch stunned as a puny white ball careers disobediently into remote shrubs and ponds, would test the patience of a Stonewall Jackson.

Viv is not quite that patient. Nor does he find such pleasure in searching for golf balls (some say he would struggle to find a haystack in a needle). Should the ball vanish into a nearby farm it will be berated by a series of unjust insults. Another ball will be teed up and it will suffer wretchedly for the sins of its predecessor. A five-iron will send it 250 yards (in Richards' golf, distance and club are not closely related: if he middles, it travels) in one direction or another. If the ball sails high and handsome, belief in the rightness of the world will be restored; if not, another tongue-in-the-cheek blast rents the air. Of course it should not be imagined that Smokey cuts a less impressive figure than Jack Nicklaus on the golf course, any more than he would appear overshadowed by Pelé on the soccer field. His air of nonchalant confidence, supported by bursts of brilliance, ensures that he bestrides whatever sport he plays.

In all that he does Richards has style. He possesses that elusive ability to appear in complete command despite overwhelming evidence to the contrary. With his enjoyment of life, Viv assumes the role of the sporting giant with relish. He drives fast cars and dresses superbly (though, strangely, most of his friends dress like sacks of potatoes). He enjoys the night-spots, plays golf and attracts such hordes of beautiful young ladies that most at Somerset feel, like Lazarus, happy to feed off the scraps from the rich man's table.

Yet for all his charm and style Viv Richards remains a private person, with a deep sense of loyalty to a few chosen and tried friends. He spends many evenings at the house of his friends, Peter and Eeva McCombe, who first took Viv in when he arrived in England in 1974. He'll chat endlessly about his days in Antigua, his years as a schoolboy and the friends of his youth. Smokey's recollections are precise and hilarious. He holds his intimate audience for hours on end. And if he teams up with Joel Garner to chatter about olden times the laughter will be uproarious – from the West Indians at least. No Englishman can fathom the lingo! At home in Antigua, Viv's house is open to guests, who range from the Prime Minister of the Island to the dustbin-man. All are received with the same grace.

Viv rarely gives vent to his strong views; his innermost beliefs remain hidden from all but his small circle of friends. Consequently his anger at injustice and prejudice surprises those who know only his ready smile. He has the presence, the personality and the discretion to emerge as an impressive and weighty ambassador for his colour and his country.

His cricket career will span a few more years yet, and he'll contribute many more virtuoso performances. In 1981 at Old Trafford he caught two astonishing catches at deep mid-wicket off successive balls, and caught them with such outrageous ease that the spectators almost took them for granted. The day before he had dropped a simple catch as he dozed quietly at slip. Upon being offered a bucket by our trainer, Dennis Waight (a brave man), he replied, 'No worries, man, I'll catch the ones that matter.' He did.

5

Combined Universities v. Yorkshire, 1976

Travelling to Barnsley, wondering why. Barnsley! Home of Parkinson and Scargill. Exams in four days time, and I'm driving up the M1 in my rickety old car on the long trek to Barnsley. We've lost all three of our Benson and Hedges games this season and have no chance of reaching the quarter-finals. We merely await the coup de grâce by a Yorkshire team who need only beat us to edge Surrey out of the competition.

We've played badly this year, a disappointment after astonishing successes against Worcester and Northants in 1975. Those victories, startlingly, all but took us into the quarter-finals. We lost narrowly at Leicester, having reduced them to 2 for 2 chasing 190, only to see Chris Balderstone survive a blatant edge to the 'keeper. He carried on to win the game for his team. Ah well, the fortunes of war! Imran Khan carried us on his broad shoulders that year, and with his loss our strike force has gone. Still, we have a talented array of batsmen, Tavaré, Parker, Marks, Roebuck and Gajan Pathmanathan, our wayward Sri Lankan gentleman. Our bowling is a bit suspect, though Gurr can be hasty and Marks bowls off-spin with a perplexed air disguising a lot of guile. And we hear Geoffrey Boycott is injured, which cheers us up no end.

Lovely meal in Barnsley at the hospitable Royal Hotel. Steaks all round. We don't have a team meeting – there's nothing much to say. Bowl straight and bat straight. We do ask our Yorkshire 2nd XI contingent, Murrills and Coverdale ('Brian'), to define the particular merits of the Tyke bowlers. Brian informs us that Chris Old 'moves the ball both ways, in the air and off the pitch, varies his pace very well and bowls a vicious bouncer'. As we sink deeper into our chairs Brian rambles on, attributing similar abilities to Oldham, Ramage, Cooper and Robinson. Gradually it dawns on us that Brian believes to the very depth of his soul that the heroes of his youth are utterly infallible. We realise, too late, that he may not have been the wisest choice to build the confidence of our thoroughly distraught batsmen. Barnsley is a long way from home!

Blue skies herald a cheerful morning as the sun rises beyond the red-brick, intimate houses of Barnsley which provide a sharp contrast to the rural poise of Cambridge. Off we go to the ground, threading through streets not cobbled these days but still narrow. The ground is small, far from beautiful, yet containing the personality of the area. Rather like Scarborough, it's a bowl surrounded by stands with red houses and television aerials peering over them. Already those stands are full to capacity, the Romans are in to witness the lions massacring the Christians. We feel a little shy as we stroll as casually as we can to inspect the pitch. It appears flat but tinged with green. Brian Close has tipped us the wink to field first at Barnsley, saying, 'It seams around a bit in t'morning, lad.'

Yorkshire appear confident, though possibly they sense a measure of nakedness without Boycott. They omit Cope and Carrick, much to our delight. As students we lack the confidence to attack spin but feel competent to nibble away at medium-pace. Marks (it's Oxford's turn to be captain!) wins the toss. To their evident surprise Yorkshire are asked to bat. Possibly this surprise thrusts their doubts to the surface.

Athey and Leadbeater stride out to bat before a packed, partisan crowd. Gurr and Brooker open the attack. Both bowl very straight. Sadly, later that season David Gurr lost confidence, spraying deliveries hither and thither, so much so that one Kent player, upon hearing that Gurr intended to head for home along the M4, commented, 'You should be all right, it's got three lanes!'

Athey, young and frail, scratches around, daunted by the thought of being stand-in for the great 'Sir Geoffrey', desperately trying to impress his audience. It's much easier for us, we don't care how we make our runs so long as we make 'em. We're not inhibited by the harsh technical insights of the Barnsley crowd. Mutters of 'He plays across t'line, tha knows' worry us not a jot. Poor Athey must show that he can bat properly, in the tradition of Hutton and Sutcliffe.

Fourteen overs bring only 17 runs. Murmurs slide around the ground. Too slow. Encouraging for us, though we'd like to rattle them with a couple of wickets. A change of bowling. A grave voice announces, 'From the river end, A. R. Wingfield-Digby.' This is more the sort of thing the crowd expected, and draws ironic cheers. A fine, double-barrelled name from the University boys – should see some leather fly. They settle into their seats, content at last.

'Wingers-Diggers' plays up to it, of course. We're only thankful he's not wearing a cravat and striped cap. There's a streak of, shall we say, eccentricity in the Wingfield-Digby blood. Several Digbys litter the tapestry of cricket, each performing his various tasks in remarkable fashion. Andrew is a good man to have in the team, always liable to pluck a startled rabbit even from the cloth cap of these parts. His bowling looks innocuous, indeed palpably innocuous, but as the ball floats down it contains sufficient cunning to trap the unwary. Eddie Barlow fell first ball to 'Diggers', caught in the gulley much to his evident dismay. Digby does have one enormous advantage over lesser mortals: as a man of the cloth he can summon formidable powers to his assistance. Sadly, he failed to contribute to *The Times* debate upon the value of praying for sporting success. With his improbable triumphs to describe he could have converted the nation with one letter!

Anyhow, our Reverend trundles up to bowl his loosener. A shade short (atheists call 'em long hops), it causes Leadbeater to essay a hook to the mid-wicket boundary. He succeeds only in edging it onto his stumps. Well, there you are, you see.

Yorkshire send in Old next. To combat the threat of Digby, or to plunder those meek outswingers? First ball he pushes forward and is rapped on the pad. Digby turns on the umpire with evangelical zeal but the umpire says 'No'. Obviously he's very sure of his place in the hereafter, for better or worse.

The crowd is quiet, the joke is wearing thin. Next ball Old again pushes vaguely forward, is struck plumb in front and sent on his way.

17 for 2 in the fifteenth over. We are enjoying ourselves hugely, surprised at the timidity of the hardened professionals. Colin Johnson joins Athey. Mark bowls very tidily to a keen field. Overs tick by, Athey strains at the leash. He hunts for runs.

We introduce our fifth bowler, R. Le Q. Savage. The Tannoy announces his name to more cheers. 'R. Le Q. Savage and Wingfield-Digby in tandem,' whisper nonplussed Yorkshire supporters. 'Oh come on, lads, this is getting serious.'

Athey falls, and acting captain John Hampshire walks in to sort out all this nonsense. A player of quality, John could turn this game in half an hour. He defends his first two balls from Savage, then drives to me at mid-on. Suddenly he charges for a desperate single. I hit the stumps and Hampshire is gone. Old and Hampshire both in the pavilion without scoring. Strange game, cricket.

67 for 4 in 28 overs. Tension grips the air. There are no derogatory shouts now, it's a scrap between equals. Johnson and Squires rebuild the innings, and Yorkshire lunch at 98 for 4 in 38 overs: an uncomfortable position for a team, in front of demanding spectators, that knows it should crush these dogged opponents.

After lunch things go badly awry, as they sometimes will. Someone manages to kick four overthrows. This cheers the crowd, who sense that we are rattled. Yorkshire gather momentum but the spurt is halted by the dismissal of Johnson and Squires. Ebbs and flows after that carry Yorkshire to a solid 185. We feel capable of passing that, given a little luck.

Such is our lack of planning that we discuss our most effective opening partnership as we leave the field. I'll have to open, but with whom? The dour Yorkie, Coverdale, or our cheery Colonial, Pathmanathan? Well, it's our last game together and we might as well enjoy it, so Pathmanathan is asked to open. Gaj and I make our way to the middle, walking together through the bank of steps in the members' stand, trying to look like Ranjitsinhji and Fry.

I tickle the first ball to long leg. Old launches into Pathmanathan, steaming down the slope in the hope of intimidating our diminutive Sri Lankan. His first bouncer disappears, with a whip of wrists, over mid-wicket, his next over square leg. Old pounds in, pitches up, and is driven back over his head with a quiet smile. 13 for 0 in one over! What on earth is happening? Dour professionals, used to defending cautiously against the new ball, stealing a single here, deflecting another there, have never witnessed this sort of nonsense before.

I block away at the other end like a good 'un, trying to restore a measure of sanity. But Gaj has the bit between his teeth. There's not much I can do about it – trench warfare is finished, the cavalry is here. I potter down between overs, advising discretion, to no avail. Pathmanathan proceeds to demolish the Yorkshire attack with unrestrained brilliance. Chris Old's figures are 0 for 36 in four overs, and he's bowled quite a few balls to me!

Astonishingly, we reach 82 in 14 overs. Yorkshire are stunned. Confusion rages. No-one knows who to bowl, where to bowl or what to bowl. It's Gaj's day and no battery of medium-pacers can upset him. Spectators start shouting. 'C'mon, Yorkshire, they're only amateurs,' cries one. Few Coke cans rattle – Barnsley is a quiet place.

Our bubble bursts. Pathmanathan and I are dismissed by Cooper. Marks and Tavaré hang on till tea, taken with Oxbridge on 98 for 2 in 25 overs. The score filters through to disbelieving ears at The Oval. Surrey have written off their chances of qualifying. After all, Yorkshire have only to beat the boys.

Yorkshire return to the fray with grim determination, fuelled by Boycott's stern presence in their dressing room. Marks and Tavaré play carefully, realising that Yorkshire must bowl us out to win: we have plenty of time to score the necessary runs. Of our batsmen to come only Parker is reliable. Coverdale and Murrills are white as sheets, not able to grasp the possibility of their heroes losing. After that, only the legendary figure of Wingfield-Digby offers hope. Our tail might wag, but then pigs might fly.

Marks and Tavaré hold firm, the thrust is resisted. By the time Tavaré is out the crowd is profoundly silent, as if awed that Yorkshire could plunge to such depths. Parker joins Marks, who cuts loose, driving Oldham over mid-off. As defeat becomes inevitable the crowds slip away, shamefacedly. Cricket means a lot up here and this defeat will linger long in the memory. Only the members remain, to offer generous applause as Parker clips the winning runs.

Jackie Hampshire, a Yorkshireman through and through, manages a brave 'well played' and Geoffrey Boycott says that when he wished us good luck he hadn't meant 'that much bloody luck'. We clamber into rattly cars for the long journey back to Cambridge and Oxford. Thoroughly revitalised, nothing thrown at us by the cruellest examiner could worry us one jot now.

Combined Universities v. Yorkshire, 1976

B. Leadbeater	b Wingfield-Digby	24
C. W. J. Athey	c Tavaré b Marks	30
C. M. Old	lbw Wingfield-Digby	0
C. Johnson	c Coverdale b Brooker	44
J. H. Hampshire	run out	0
P. J. Squires	c Roebuck b Brooker	27
D. L. Bairstow	c Coverdale b Brooker	18
A. Ramage	not out	17
H. P. Cooper	not out	3
Extras		22
		——
Total (7 wkts, 55 overs)		185

Did not bat: S. Oldham, A. L. Robinson.
Fall of wickets: 1–53, 2–53, 3–67, 4–67, 5–130, 6–144, 7–167.
Bowling: Gurr 11–4–23–0; Brooker 11–4–44–3; Savage 11–1–40–0;
Marks 11–3–22–1; Wingfield-Digby 11–1–34–2.

COMBINED UNIVERSITIES

P. M. Roebuck	c Bairstow b Cooper	22
G. Pathmanathan	c Johnson b Cooper	58
C. J. Tavaré	lbw Oldham	33
V. J. Marks	not out	47
P. W. G. Parker	not out	19
Extras		7
		——
Total (3 wkts, 47 overs)		186

Did not bat: S. P. Coverdale, T. J. Murrills, A. R. Wingfield-Digby,
R. Le Q. Savage, D. Gurr, M. E. W. Brooker.
Fall of wickets: 1–82, 2–83, 3–136.
Bowling: Old 7–0–45–0; Robinson 11–1–29–0; Cooper 11–1–52–2;
Oldham 11–1–32–1; Ramage 7–1–21–0.
Combined Universities won by 7 wkts.

6

'Trout'

As I write this, the sun sinks behind the Opera House and the Harbour Bridge. Sydney prepares for night. Today another illusion was shattered. Today John Barclay, a noted and admired blocker, a worthy member of Stonewall Jackson's Army, scored 95 in 79 minutes. Can nothing be relied upon in these changing times? Where will it all end? Soon we'll discover that John Wayne really spoke with a falsetto voice or that W. G. Grace's beard was stuck on. 95 in 79 minutes!

John Robert Troutbeck Barclay. 'Trout'. Eton, MCC and Sussex. Upright, courageous, friendly, well-spoken: all the trimmings of the Old Etonian. But dour, dogged, defensive, determined and, from time to time, dull, too. The Grenadier Guard hammering it out in the trenches as a trooper, with the language, the sweat, the dirt and the tarts (not that Trout is ever dirty, it's the troopers I'm talking about, you understand). An odd mixture is Sussex's captain. Pedestrian John Barclay and flamboyant Robert Troutbeck. So many of our most honoured leaders have had suppressive names, could they have succeeded without them? Winston Churchill, Napoleon, Boadicea, Attila the Hun, Hagar the Horrible. Surely Bob the Hun or Anthony the Horrible dare not have behaved so barbarically?

Anyhow, Trout was captain of Sussex at the tender age of 27. Despite his lack of years, John has a wealth of experience to support him in his task. At Hove he has played under Tony Greig and Arnold 'Ob' Long, and with Wessels, Snow, Imran, le Roux and Javed Miandad ('the only father-son relationship in modern cricket'!). He has toured South Africa, Australia, Canada and the Far East. He'll need these foundations if he is to thrive.

It helps, too, that he is an optimist. Sussex's finances crumble and crash, with apparently only the age-old pensioners in their deck chairs keeping ruin at bay. Trout is working to rejuvenate the sagging morale at his club, and to produce a strong and thriving cricket team to stimulate interest. His chances of success are helped by his calm, tolerant personality. John's only similarity to Karl Marx is that he sees the world as divided into two sorts of people. With John there are 'nice chaps' and 'fairly nice chaps'. Al Capone on St Valentine's Day, or Stalin in one of his less liberal moods, might require the 'fairly' to be spoken very slowly, otherwise condemnation is not a part of Barclay's conversations.

John is a most amiable individual, the Julie Andrews of cricket. Colleagues struggle to think of any vice from which he suffers. It is whispered abroad that he does not quite always walk, and he has been known to utter oaths upon particular misfortunes, but you can tell that his heart is not really in it and that he expects the wrath of God to singe his hair at any moment. Well, you can't imagine Julie Andrews barring the way with Marlene Dietrich in some shady Berlin night club, can you?

He's not perfect, of course. For a start he talks all the time, usually about cricket. He's not one of those Etonians who are men of actions, not words, the sort who lead the cavalry charge or climb Mount Everest on a kangaroo without puttin' a wisp of hair out of place. No, Trout may be heroic but he is rarely silent. He rambles on, pausing only for breath, during which you may scamper in with a wise word or two, before merrily continuing where he left off. And once an idea is lodged in his mind it stays there for a long time, for there is a stubborn streak in Barclay which has riled barrackers from Truro to Ottawa. Like 'Barnacle' Bailey, Trout bats as if there were a crisis, if not present most certainly looming. Probably he'd make a nifty Chancellor of the Exchequer. For despite his amiable manner, John Barclay is a most dedicated and determined cricketer. He has a measure of stoicism that impresses his peers, while his unaffected manner, and willingness to shrug off the limelight to team-mates, are popular with fellow-professionals.

John is known for his courage, especially for his ability to cope with the 'hairy quicks' as they roar down the slope at Hove of a misty morning. He moves into line with utter discipline, as might Paynter or Leyland of old, recalling the adage, 'None of us likes fast bowling, but some of us don't show it'. Not all cricketers regard fast bowling as a challenge, a test of manhood. I well remember Mervyn Kitchen being hit on the knee by a Wes Hall full toss: he hopped, jumped and stomped, frolicking around like a lamb in spring (though his language was rather less discreet). And in the same game Chris Greetham walked majestically after a Hall bouncer flew past his glove. Ken Palmer shouted down to him, 'You never hit that, Greeth' to which our thoroughly sane hero replied, 'Near enough for me, Ken. Good morning.'

Undoubtedly John is at his best against fast bowling. He is not a powerful man, nor a gifted timer of the ball, but he relies on cuts, square drives and deflections to bring a consistent stream of runs. These shots are most easily played using the pace of the ball, as Barclay ably demonstrated in his innings in Sussex's 1978 Gillette Cup triumph when he repeatedly square cut Garner to the boundary. With stern defence he can resist the onslaught so that more wide-ranging batsmen can flourish in less hazardous circumstances. If Trout does survive the new ball, and he often does, his limitations become more obvious. Far less threatening bowlers can subdue him for long periods, supported by defensive fields, especially if they angle the ball into his pads.

In a long innings, Trout's scoring rate increases slowly. Consequently his irreverent team-mates follow a Barclay innings as a golfer marks his card. If John is 26 after 28 overs he is said to be '2 under par', and if he is 47 after 44 overs he is '3 over par'. Only once before today has Trout thrown this rule of thumb into disarray. Returning from injury, he struck 16 runs against Glamorgan off Ezra Moseley's opening over. Needless to say he fell soon after, and deservedly so, for one cannot defy one's gods so much. Geoff Arnold rushed to the Sussex dressing room to see whether Barclay's health, mental and physical, had suffered some terrible relapse.

It will not be a surprise by now to hear that Barclay has never hit a six in county cricket. Rumours spread by the Welsh suggest a possibility that he once cleared the ropes at Cardiff in the dim past, but these reports are hazy and unconfirmed and are regarded as no more reliable than the hoteliers around Loch Ness sighting a massive, scaly monster. Incidentally, it took Brian Rose six years to hit his first six, upon which he hit two more in the same over. I hope Trout is never captured by the flavour of the big hit: some things are not meant to be.

But John is more than a mere batsman. He bowls his off-spin with an intelligent and quizzical air. His flight and guile are used only sporadically at Brighton, but bowling on such a discouraging surface has encouraged mastery of line and length with small, subtle variations to disturb the batsman who presumes too much. Often he proves to be Sussex's most economical bowler in Sunday games – no doubt a reward for bowling straight.

John's contests with Ian Botham are usually particularly spectacular. As different as chalk and cheese, these men somehow provoke each other into friendly conflict. Botham regards Barclay's Etonian accent, generous flight and perplexed manner as a challenge not to be resisted. No sooner does Botham stroll hugely to the crease, swinging his arms to loosen his limbs for the plunder ahead, than Barclay comes on to bowl. The battle rarely lasts long, though casualties can be considerable in the meantime, and ends when another very slow delivery is sent soaring into the air with a depressed fieldsman, who'd probably spilt his coffee that morning, under it. Yet the contest does not finish there. John Barclay, a most rational and pragmatic cricketer, for obscure reasons cannot resist the temptation of Botham's bouncer and has been caught at long leg several times. The Roundheads do not always defeat the Cavaliers.

As a fielder, Trout is superb at first slip. He catches the ball wonderfully well. Whereas some of us hang on to it as a stranded whale hangs on to life, Barclay's hands appear to act in sympathy with the ball which lands in them and stays there as if it had found at last a roof that did not leak. His outfielding is more sedate. He remembers running out Dennis Breakwell in 1976. Since Dennis's playing name alternated from 'The severed nerve' to 'Twitch', his run-out is less surprising than John's ability to recall it five years later. Can it be that those monks who can speak only once every seven years (which, by the way, is an excellent qualification for discussing cricket with John!) remember their conversations for similar reasons?

Alas, as ever, a mere recital of the performance of a most capable professional cricketer fails to capture the essence of the man. Trout has a deep love of cricket. He travels the world in the winter, coaching and playing. At Waverley (before his outrageous 95 in 79 minutes) we coached young Australians together, thereby damning Aussie cricket to obscurity for a generation. I well recall one Oliver Banks (6), after

31

witnessing a vivid demonstration of the hook by Mr Barclay, whispering to his mates, 'Ah! That's the shot I play every ball!' The highlight of each day was the great match, Mr Barclay's XI against Mr Roebuck's XI. This invariably resulted in bedlam, with children flying in all directions, overthrows, cover shots, run-outs, wides, byes and Trout yelling 'This is incredibly exciting!', 'Brilliant stop!', 'Heroic dive!' or whatever else sprang to mind amidst the chaos. Trout regarded it as a profound personal challenge that each contest should end as a dramatic tie, and we recorded 19 ties in succession! Without wishing to shatter whatever illusions survive Barclay's 95, I fear these things can be engineered, for six-year-old children do not notice if the score conveniently leaps from 17 to 53 after a quiet tickle to long leg.

By degrees our courses became more famous and more insane. At first Trout and I would roar 'Catch!' or 'Dive!' or 'Jump!' or 'Run!' after each ball, to stimulate excitement. Eventually we decided to save our voices by appointing someone to shout 'Catch!', someone else to bellow 'Dive!' and so on every ball. By the end of the month we had kids, desperate for a role, roaring 'Swim!' and 'Check!', which did rather add to the confusion. Quite what the parents made of it all I don't know – put it down to English eccentricity, I suppose.

After four weeks of these exhausting courses John and I repaired to Waverley for a nice, quiet game of cricket. You can guess the rest: Trout made a sporting declaration, and we ended up in another desperate finish with everyone yelling at everyone else, with appeals, overthrows and dropped catches punctuating the tense atmosphere. It all exactly resembled the youngsters' games about which we had smiled so knowingly for a month.

7

In Fiji

They have some strange customs in Fiji, as I realised during my visit there. As usual I did not learn my lesson quite quickly enough to avoid trouble! After a day's cricket we repaired to a nearby tin shack, perched precariously on stilts, for a few drinks to whet our appetite for supper. A pig was smoking (not idly inhaling a Havana but roasting on a spit: I daresay the pig would have preferred the cigar). We sipped at our whisky with developing enthusiasm. To be honest, I mistrust the stuff; I've watched too many W. C. Fields films to feel at ease with it. Still, Fiji is a long way from home and they were downing scotches like Humphrey Bogart. These Fijians are men's men, built like Charles Bronson, moustache and all, and if they drink you must do so, too.

Although we had few words in common, conversation flourished as the scotch nagged away at empty stomachs, and with shrewd use of limbs, grunts and groans we were quickly deep in debate. It resembled one of those spaghetti westerns with Clint Eastwood and Lee Van Cleef in which growls, snarls and flickers express profound emotion. Eventually, I'm forced to concede, the pangs of hunger led me to deny my upbringing by asking whether the pig might not be well done by now. After all, we'd been sipping and chatting for hours, and I'd not eaten since that gigantic breakfast at half-noon (by this stage I was affecting a manner of expressing time reliant upon observation rather than Seiko, and drawn largely from Geronimo). And as we appeared to have two moons now, and as my stomach was rumbling, might we not bang the gong? Immediately they sprang to their feet. After a few wobbles they intimated that they'd been waiting for two hours for me to say I was hungry. Apparently in Fiji it is considered rude to dine until the guest gives the nod. With our different customs we could have been there all night.

33

My visit to Fiji was a trip into the unknown. I doubt if even Bing Crosby and Bob Hope ever went on the road there, from an advanced material society to subsistence farming. Living in tin shacks, without fridges or TV, was a way of life. Yet no-one complained of hardship, all were well fed. No-one appeared to be worried about anything although the Indian population, who want things to run on time, looked weary. The Fijians can be startlingly unreliable. If you arrange a match to begin at 2 pm you might, with a little luck, find eight players by 3 pm. Everyone will be immensely cheerful, sitting in the shade as the heat of the day passes. As you fret, they smile. Maybe they had found something better to do. Replacements are easy to find. Nip out to the road, hail the first passing Pacific Islander (the Indians take business more seriously) and enquire whether he fancies a game of cricket? 'Sure,' he replies, delighted, and, after a pause, 'What's cricket?'

Usually these men, even the novices, contribute something to the game. Superb athletes with massive shoulders, they all field well and throw ferociously. It must be those strange root vegetables. At the wicket they will probably swipe a couple of mighty blows before laughing uproariously as their stumps are spreadeagled.

It's a pity, with this zest and delight, that cricket is dying in Fiji. It has lost the enthusiasm and drive brought by the missionaries long ago. In older days Fiji could visit New Zealand, as they did in 1948, and hold their own with provincial teams. Even now the most senior cricketers bat with skill, evidently well coached in the techniques of the science. Alas, most of the youngsters are keen but undisciplined, in need of a stern grounding in fundamentals. These youngsters might do well in familiar conditions, but they struggle abroad. In the 1979 mini-World Cup, Fiji brought a talented native team which fared very badly. Of course the bitter, damp weather did not help. Nor did the novelty of playing on grass and wearing cricket boots. Malo Bula, a whimsical off-spinner, wore cricket whites for the first time in Shrewsbury – previously he had preferred his native Sulu dress. Not many Fijians wear Sulus, even though its thick cloth renders pads virtually unnecessary. Most wear more orthodox attire, but nevertheless first-class cricketers' eyebrows would bobble up and down at the implements used in Fiji. Batsmen wear no helmet or visor, chest protectors are not thought to be essential. Gloves are too expensive and are scorned anyway. Several men, facing bowlers of, say, Hendrick's pace, not only foreswear helmets and gloves but wear no shoes or socks either! A riveting sight.

Malo is quite a character, by the way, a cunning bowler who laughs and fools around too much to be a regular in his national side. A Fijian Ray East. To be too unreliable for Fiji! It's a bit like being rejected by Attila for being too wild.

Although cricket is battling to survive on the biggest islands of the Fiji group, it is thriving in one small and remote isle, Lakeba. Lakeba has a population of 2,500 comprising 32 different tribes. It is the home of Fiji's Prime Minister, Ratu Sir Kamisese Mara. Being a wise man, Sir Kamisese has forbidden the playing of rugby in Lakeba, since it caused far too many tribal injuries – a most judicious move, which the Welsh might bear in mind! Cricket, he felt, might result in less open warfare. So it was to Lakeba I flew, landing on a minute strip of sand, to see Fijian cricket at its best. Lakeba is a mixture of communal farming and mediaeval crafts. Each family has its role in the island's subsistence economy. One family organises everything, another traditionally runs the shop, another has always distributed the food, and everyone takes his turn working in the fields.

It is an unusual island, an improbable nest of cricket. The shy inhabitants stick together, reluctant to accompany outsiders in the Fiji team, proud of their heritage. Attitudes are similar to those found in Barbados, as the great traditions breed insularity. Mind you, Lakeba is not so very different from the rest of Fiji. It, too, runs to a mysterious concept known as 'Fiji time'. This requires everyone to be at least two hours late. Every once in a while, though, and without any apparent signal, everyone must be half an hour early, just to show who is boss. It's a strange notion, inaccessible to guests, and you end up puzzled, shrugging your shoulders.

Matches in Lakeba are an event, the event to which every inhabitant looks forward. No need for ritual dances when you can appeal for lbw, no value in witch doctors when umpires and scorers are available. The whole island turns out for the games, played on Wednesdays (Sundays are reserved for less solemn religions). And, as one wide-eyed child put it, 'We all come, the blind, the crazy – even the teachers!' At first, dull-witted authorities in Suva decreed with dire threats that schools in Lakeba must stay open on Wednesdays. But no-one ever turned up, so, defeated, the Government withdrew gracefully.

The pitch is set, in village-green style, amongst the huts in which the locals live. Ratu Sir Kamisese Mara's house dominates one boundary and the sparkling Pacific laps into the palm trees on another. Lakebans sit under the palms skirting the ground, cheering, laughing, clapping. Heroes are not taken too seriously, not when you harvest alongside them in the fields. The pitch itself is made of concrete, covered by a thin green canvas. It is a reliable surface, encouraging batsmen to swing through the line. The ocean breeze assists swing-bowling. Nothing is done to aid spinners, for boundaries are short and canvas unreceptive. But then, visiting teams invariably rely on spin while Lakeba are stronger in pace and movement.

Incidentally, innocent visiting teams must be careful in these parts, must define the rules of the game with the utmost attention to detail. One team, en route to Lakeba, stopped on a nearby island for a quick game. Alas they did not realise that playing the island involved playing the *whole* island, men, women and children. People kept cheerfully strapping on pads and striding out to bat. No-one had the slightest idea how to swing a bat but every inhabitant wanted a go. It proved to be a long fielding session. You try to dismiss 170 men, women and children in an evening.

(Actually, novel views of cricket are not uniquely Fijian. Joe Hillaire, a colleague of mine at Cranbrook School, Sydney, believed that byes should not count since 'ze man did not hit ze ball'. Joe also kept score in a refreshingly different way. With Joe 3 for 48 meant you had dismissed three batsmen from 48 balls! George Gassman, our German teacher, on the other hand advised his lowly team to use the back of the bat so that the fielders would not know which way the ball was going! Meanwhile K. J. Lee, the resident Japanese, never could see quite why he needed to umpire from behind the stumps. Far more fun to stroll around the field, giving decisions from a variety of angles!)

Cricket is not nearly so distinctive in Lakeba. The proud Island team holds the national shield and most decidedly intends to keep it. The great hero, and a cricketer of explosive talent, is Peni Dakai. Peni resembles Andy Roberts, with his powerful shoulders and steely blue eyes. But though he does open the bowling with his swingers, his reputation rests on his batting, which can be as destructive as that of Roberts' Antiguan colleague, Vivian Richards. Peni hits the ball very, very hard. He lives at deep mid-wicket, which is appropriate enough, though he prefers to drive the ball over the trees into the ocean 100 yards away. His record in Lakeba includes several rapid centuries against reputable clubs. In England he was ever cold and depressed and gave only glimpses of his prowess. He survived only four balls against Bangladesh, but that was enough time for a 'sighter', a four and a skimming, straight six that almost broke the sight-screen. Peni is a hitter, not a slogger: like Richards, he uses a short back-lift and is a dangerous, powerful opponent. Had Dakai been born in a more mature cricketing country he might well have brightened our lives. How many other cricketers of genius are scattered around the world, unrecognised?

Despite the mysteries of Fiji time and mountainous English breakfasts, I survived my trip to Lakeba. I fear I resembled Sir Stafford Cripps in my coaching, though, as I tried to persuade these huge men to hit straight rather than to cow-shot corner (a phrase that took some explaining). At least I made no effort to restrict their natural joy in 'beating the ball'.

By the way, the smoked pig was delicious and the root vegetables restored my sorely tested strength. And I enjoyed the whisky, too!

8

Three Men In A Car

On the road again! Three weary wanderers darting from Folkestone to Taunton to sleep, sweet sleep. Our evenings are spent in cars, chatting, dozing, tripping with headphones or scratchily studying mysterious maps. Each summer I drive 12,000 miles up and down the country on motorways and country lanes, 240 hours at the wheel every season and often after a full day's cricket!

Vic Marks, Richard Ollis and I travel in my Renault crossing the busy country. They are my normal companions, originally chosen for their sparkling wit to help while away the hours. Alas, on our first journey from Taunton to Leicester they both fell sound asleep by Weston-super-Mare (one thinks on motorways in terms not of time but of signposts) and visions of pleasant conversations were rapidly abandoned. But my friends were wide awake by Worcester and have not slept much since. The reason was the battle-scarred VW I was driving in those days. It jumped and choked past Worcester like a Grand National horse with a lady jockey. It simply refused to contemplate third or first gear. It tolerated fourth and second only if they were crashed and the gearstick held firmly in place. What with the jams and my fierce arguments with the car, Vic and Richard could no more sleep than could Macbeth (another man tormented by a female driver). We made it to Leicester amidst some vivid cursing. Three days later, I returned alone ahead of my team-mates lest I break down. For obscure reasons this time the car would accept only third and second and I spent a wearing journey gripping the reluctant gears in place. I reached Taunton tired and cross but in far better health than the car.

As Richard and Vic soon learned, the old VW had a broken sun-roof, too. Whilst it never opened itself to the sun's warm rays, it was quite happy to allow the rains to pour through upon driver and crew.

I drove home from Lord's in 1978 wrapped in pinched towels (sorry, Mr Allen), in two inches of water and with a torrent flooding down my shoulders, feeling like Noah. My old VW has gone now, like a prostitute, into dishonourable retirement. It was fun while it lasted!

Vic, Ollis and I are at least dry in my Renault. It's a long journey home, fully 4½ hours. I'll drive most of the way and Vic will relieve me for a while in the middle. Though the car is reliable, our knowledge of directions is not. Richard Ollis, a lad brought up in Keynsham where he has since remained, feels that on reaching London we should turn left at the first set of lights. But this same Richard had been astonished by how bright the lights of Soho were at midnight compared to those in Keynsham, so we confidently ignore his Lieutenant Phillips-like navigational contributions (and it's no business of yours what we were doing in Soho at midnight). Vic, on the other hand, a wily old bird, reckons he knows a back way, avoiding the dreaded South Circular. He'll guide me through a maze of B-roads, he says.

But I've travelled with 'Vic-lad' for eight years. A gentle, humorous soul, he's liable to miss his way in a car park. In eight years we've scarcely ever agreed on which turn to make at a cross-roads. On one historic occasion we contrived to leave Bristol by its northern fringes when we should have been heading in the general direction of Taunton. Another time we passed through the Blackwall tunnel three times, each time passing an old lady walking along the road, who studied our furious progress with interest. Travelling to Folkestone in thick mist, we've even managed to circle round a roundabout several times, hunting for hidden signposts and slip-roads. Roundabouts are awkward in mist; as they have no cat's eyes, you never know how round the about is.

We plod along, desperate to reach the blessed relief of the motorway as soon as possible – so many fewer decisions to make on motorways, less concentration required of tired brains. Richard, Vic and I settle down for the journey. I switch on the radio, listen to the World Service or Radio 4, anything to avoid the monotony of the Test match in which Boycott and Tavaré are fighting a noble rearguard action. We follow a drama about an artist, a tortured genius (I ask Vic if he is a tortured genius and he replies, 'Only when they sweep my arm ball'), who eventually is successful. Immediately he commits suicide.

Apparently his devoted wife had painted his famous portraits and he was ashamed to admit it. All good, stirring stuff to pass the evening.

We plough on, frustrated by women drivers evidently popping out to see their maiden aunts or doddery old oafs ambling along, enjoying the scenery. We have a long way to go to get home and it was a gruelling afternoon in the field, not a recipe for patient tolerance. I nip out to overtake and Vic says we'll make it – with a little luck and God willing!

We approach the motorway. Should we have a bite now, wait until a service station beckons or slip off the motorway into the comforts of a West Country pub? We decide on the last, as the service stations south of the Trent are too terrible to contemplate. Vic takes the wheel for a while. Vic is a rural driver oblivious to others, jogging along without a care in the world, without indicators or mirrors. We are lucky if he notices anything more than 20 yards in front, apart maybe from a herd of cows. Vic's never quite sure whether to overtake or not, peering out of the side window to see if the coast is clear – and I use the word 'coast' advisedly. If it's not clear as far as Dover, we'll stay right where we are and Vic will start growling. He'll bravely ignore my 'Don't dither, Vic', 'Attack, Vic, attack' and 'That cyclist is catching us up' with brooding eyes. Eventually, driven to distraction, he announces 'All right, you buggers, I'm off', at which point Richard and I dive for cover, raising our eyes to peep over the bonnet seconds later with the cunning glint of Tom pleased to have evaded the big dog.

To endure Vic's spasmodic driving, we switch on *Brain of Britain*. My old maths teacher once entered this illustrious competition, giving answers that were always speculatively inspired and invariably mistaken. They sounded so convincing that one began to suspect Robert Robinson must have a dud encyclopedia. Neither Vic nor I succeed, despite our groundings in classics and law. They never quite ask any questions within our field, which is admittedly somewhat narrow, limited as it is to Somerset's opening batsmen in the 1970s. Still, we have much fun explaining how we knew the answer really but simply didn't have time to blurt it out. As we listen, so Vic's driving loses every ounce of aggression. He is utterly unable to attack at the wheel whilst turning over in his mind various improbable solutions to tricky questions.

At last we reach the motorway, after a vital right turn at the

Thames, observed by Richard Ollis. I resume the hot seat for the rush at the motorway and it's full steam ahead, 90 miles an hour all the way or 70 if you are a policeman. Several Somerset cars will pass me, though I expect they have lost their way. Since I arrived at Folkestone one hour before anyone else they really ought to have listened to my advice on the best route; as Viv had said, 'Follow the man in form, listen to the man informed.' I was running pretty hot on routes at this time but of course they'd all devised their own special ways – some men are born like barbers, with blind faith in short cuts.

Up the motorway as so often before, and by now we know exactly how many miles each motorway sign will say for Bristol and for Taunton. The M4 and the M5 hold no surprises for us. Vic offers me a Murraymint and lights a fag. Time drags, so we decide to tease young Ollis. We sigh, reflecting upon our careers, noting success and failure, admitting that we must soon abandon our chewing gum, as the younger generation pushes its way up like fresh, young grass. At least, we reflect, we can justly feel satisfied at leaving our beloved club in such secure hands as those of young Ollis in the back there. We suppose we'll struggle on for a couple more years whilst the young 'uns find their feet. Then we must depart, and gracefully, leaving the field to the exciting raw talent of these youngsters. We'll enjoy sitting under the scoreboard at Taunton, watching the new team bringing our club to greater glories. Hopefully we will not mutter too much about how things used to be when it was Richards and Botham, not Ollis and Felton. Richard is a little puzzled, not entirely convinced we are being 'straight up'. With profound sincerity he suggests we could struggle on a bit longer, as he doesn't feel quite able to take the reins just yet. He suspects he's being teased at last and informs us that we should get on with our ruddy driving and navigating.

We emerge from this interlude to find ourselves careering along the M4 towards Bristol. We approach the Frome turn-off, Gavaskar Corner. It was near here that I saw Sunil Gavaskar change colour. It's a complicated tale. Dennis Breakwell, Colin Dredge (the Demon of Frome) and I were driving our 1980 Saabs in convoy along the M4. I'd thought I was behind Breakwell who was headed for Taunton, as I was. We reached the Frome exit, the car in front went left, I automatically followed – the brain gets blurred on motorways – and suddenly I realised I was behind Colin. This was not my exit. Like

Starsky I whirled the steering wheel, sending dust and stones flying in all directions. I drove across the grass and back onto the motorway behind Breakwell. I'm afraid Gavaskar, my passenger, went very pale indeed.

10.15, nearly home, time for food. We escape into a pub for a mixed grill and a pint of best. Thank heaven for motorways – tediously predictable, but what must it have been like before them? How could WG have played cricket after a long journey in a carriage with little suspension? We bubble cheerfully on for the last few miles which somehow or other seem to take ages. As the marathon runners say, 'It's not the 26 miles that hurt, it's the 286 yards at the end.' Eventually, though, another journey is completed, we can put our feet up at home, unpack our suitcases and sleep in our own beds. Only 10,000 more miles to travel this season (rather more if Vic navigates) and it will all be over.

9

R. J. O. Meyer

It was RJO, 'Boss', who taught me an infallible cure for hiccups. We were sitting in his dingy office in Athens, chatting about S. F. Barnes, underarm bowling and Harold Gimblett. Suddenly Meyer piped up that he could cure my hiccups, and promptly did so. He'd learned the trick in India. All you have to do is . . . Ah, no – it's been a handy weapon at parties ever since, even though hiccups are caught (or is it hicked?) by robust Elsie Tanners rather than delicate Sophia Lorens.

RJO learned many things in India. He learned to live with a few hours sleep a week (shelling at night prevented more) and he realised that he must concentrate on education not on his cricket career. As for the sleep, well he beds down for an hour or two most nights these days (after all, he is 77) but rarely for longer. A few years ago he could work a 16-hour day and still find the energy to pop down to London, to the casinos or to a racecourse. His pupils saw him at a point-to-point once in a while, and would surreptitiously follow him to see which horses he backed. If Millfield's stable had two horses running in a race (one a favourite, one an outsider) the afternoon might be particularly rewarding. And as for his decision to abandon cricket for education, cricket lost an original mind. RJO regrets that decision, and warmly advised me to pursue my cricket career as far as it could go. Plenty of time for other challenges later, he reckoned.

In his brief cricket career, Boss hinted at potential in his Victorian style and approach. He was, colleagues suggest, a bit of a rogue. One season, as captain, he appeared the afternoon before the first county match and demanded a net from his professionals, who had showered and changed to drive east. Growls and groans followed, but rebellion was avoided by a timely downpour.

Boss developed endless theories about cricket, which he tried from time to time to the consternation of his dour professionals. He had plenty of imagination and plenty of will to try something different. Only five years ago he all but persuaded me of the merits of bowling underarm in the next Varsity match, pointing out that no-one would have any idea how to cope with curls, skids, floats or whatever. He showed me his range of deliveries with a tennis ball on a basketball court in Athens, an improbable setting. It seemed a good idea at the time, though when I reached the cobwebs of Lord's the novelty was hastily shelved. Boss rebuked me, too, when I played in Corfu for his school team. One Corfiote enjoyed a pleasant afternoon smiting our somewhat friendly attack over the hotels and taverna at mid-wicket. 'Why didn't you throw up a few leg-breaks?' Boss queried. 'Well, it was an overs game and we were trying to keep the runs down,' I replied shamefacedly. Ah, where has the spirit of man gone? Meyer would have tried something, anything, to buy wickets.

R. J. O. Meyer played long enough to leave his mark on the game. Stories of his idiosyncratic captaincy still circulate in Taunton. One April, apparently, as the lack of discipline and organisation the previous season had been painfully obvious, Meyer decided to arrange the field placements for each bowler before the first game, so that each man might move to his position automatically. They sat in the dressing room, with Meyer deploying his troops with the aplomb of a Montgomery. All went well in the first game at Lord's. Somerset's well-oiled machine reduced Middlesex to 80 for 5 or thereabouts. The Long Room was most impressed. 'Somerset look keen this year,' they were saying. 'Damn' good skipper, this Meyer.' Then a new man arrived and took guard. He was a left-hander. 'Oh, great thing of me forgot,' muttered Meyer. Chaos followed, with fielders scurrying around like drunken rabbits or shaking their heads sadly as temperament directed.

Meyer was not one to take established notions as read. His mind ranged free, undisturbed by ostrich-like reliance upon reduced rationality. If he thought he needed two fly-slips and a deep point, he had them. If he decided to tempt the batsmen to drive by removing mid-off and mid-on, he did so. If it struck him that the incumbent was hopeless off his pads, he put all his fielders on the off-side. All of them.

Alas, Boss was an unlucky adventurer, much as Rommel was when his camels failed him. He needed talented cricketers around him to support his inspirations and to secure the bridge if things fell apart.

He did not have them. His best-laid plans went awry through a persistent inability in his team to catch or bend. His bowlers were willing, but ploys failed as catches were spilt. Alexander the Great could not have won the Championship for Somerset in Meyer's years. The final nail was driven into the coffin the year Meyer decided to lift spirits by buying a piano for the dressing room. He approached a piano salesman (there must be a name for such people – tinklers?) and asked for a piano for his team. 'A good swop, mate,' replied the jovial tinkler, 'a good swop!'

If as a captain Boss was a little beyond his team, as a young cricketer he had considerable ability. A tall, spare man, he stood up at the crease and cracked the ball straight in the classical way. He recalls with relish his duel with S. F. Barnes ('the greatest bowler who ever lived') in a Gentlemen v. Players match. He survived, despite Barnes' tetchy cussedness. Every ball bowled by Barnes appeared at first to be a high full toss, a gift from the gods. As it fizzed down it dropped into a mere full toss, then a half-volley until, at the very instant the batsman gratefully went for his drive, it dipped wickedly into the turf to rise steeply past the shoulder of lunging bat, having cut one way or the other. Meyer admired Barnes' ability to impart swing and cut by prodigious spin, and tried in vain to persuade Lord's to film his action for the benefit of posterity. What a pity Lord's failed to heed his advice!

The other bowling action Meyer greatly praised that evening in Athens was Jeff Thomson's, with its use of a catapult arm. He suggested that Thomson would have been far more dangerous had he straightened his wrist at the moment of delivery, to encourage movement and assist accuracy. As a bowler himself (Meyer was much too easily bored to be a mere batsman, his theories could best be tested as an all-rounder), RJO bowled a variety of balls, as might be expected. He'd bowl a spinner, a seamer, a swinger or a shower ball, all designed to disturb the batsman's watchful skills or to penetrate particular defects. Apparently Boss had little use for the 'dot' ball, the Cartwright or Underwood strangulation of the batsman. He preferred to match his skill against his opponent's, to try to trap him through stealth rather than to starve him to death.

Cricket's evident loss was education's gain. To it Meyer brought his originality and enthusiasm, and founded a series of independent schools in which he was very definitely Boss. In these schools he explored his theories, gave air to his experiments. In India he had educated the sons of the Indian aristocracy. Upon his return to England he bought an old Army camp near Glastonbury and called it Millfield School. For 20 years most lessons were given in Nissen huts or 'chicken runs'. He wanted his school to be co-educational, to offer the widest possible range of activities to its pupils, and to try to release the talent in each student – in whatever direction it might lie. He attracted princes, sheikhs and actors, despite his requirement that rich parents pay massive fees so that he might accept able children of Macclesfield road-sweepers or Llanelli miners free.

He started the first dyslexia group, too, run by one A. F. Fletcher, who was originally a maths teacher. AFF was an extraordinary man, sporadically appearing on *Brain of Britain* (invariably giving answers of inaccurate genius), tramping about the school with his bike (skis, if snow fell) and old raincoat, peeping into dustbins as if they were casseroles. A. F. Fletcher taught these 'no-hopers' for two years and emerged unscathed. Later he was triumphant, as his ex-pupils inevitably became merchant bankers, civil servants, international sportsmen or crooks!

I arrived at Millfield in 1967, four years before Meyer and his school parted company in acrimonious circumstances. As I was (while young!) a good sportsman, I was advised to visit Millfield to see if I could obtain a free scholarship. My family came along, too. I knocked nervously on Boss's study door. As I entered an orange flew towards me. I caught it. 'Well done,' said Meyer, 'but you should have thrown it back.' He took me to a tennis court to bat with a tennis racquet to the bowling of my reluctant sister. Seven years later that sister captained Oxford University at cricket! The ladies' team.

Meyer not only gave me a scholarship but instructed my whole family to come to Millfield, parents to teach, children to study. He provided us with a house down the road, to ease our lives! That orange test was not his only weapon. He had several intelligence tests of the lateral thinking variety, none of which I have ever been able to disentangle without the broadest of hints.

After he left Millfield, he flew to Athens to start a new school, despite the colonels' regime of the time. I taught at his Campien School for a while and survived its boundless energy. Of course Meyer only employed me to strengthen his cricket team for its annual trip to

Corfu. Believing in the educational value of cricket, he wants to persuade the Greek authorities to form a cricket body to encourage its growth. Don't bet against it! Meyer still plays from time to time, flooring Corfiotes with his cunningly flighted spinners.

Now, at 77, he has started yet another independent school, St Lawrence's College by name. He is still scuttling to and from the Alpha-beta store in Paleo Psychcio, seeing if *The Times* is in and buying a little soup to support his angular, energetic frame for a little longer.

10

Somerset v. Essex

1978 Gillette Cup Semi-Final

Of the four teams left in the Gillette Cup, Essex and Somerset appeared the strongest. Neither club had ever won a trophy, and when they were drawn to meet each other at Taunton in the semi-final both knew that a day of truth had come. Gooch, McEwan, Fletcher and Lever facing Richards, Botham, Rose and Garner. Victory in this game must surely bring glory at last. It turned out not to be so. The giants took too much out of each other. The winner never recovered his strength to destroy lesser fry in the final. But many people remember this game as they remember the first Ali v. Frazier fight, for its drama and its twists of fortune. Possibly it was the best of all one-day cricket matches.

It was definitely the most appalling game in which I have played. Nerve-jangling, desperately hard-fought, undeserving of a loser. After the last ball the winners could scarcely believe their luck, could hardly raise sufficient energy to laugh. Both winners and losers collapsed into chairs, some of the losers shedding tears of bitter disappointment. Even the crowd, after an immediate surge of excitement, crept away in a strange silence, exhausted by the strain of the day.

The ground was teeming by 9 am, full of colour and noise. They were in the trees, on the roofs, under the sight-screens. Thousands were locked out until chairman Herbie Hoskins re-opened the gates. Many were uncomfortable. The meagre facilities could not cope with such a crowd, and hundreds could barely see the middle. But no-one minded, it was not a day for complaint.

Brian Rose won the toss and surprised his team by batting.

Somerset's usual policy was to chase runs, relying on a powerful batting line-up. But this was a semi-final. Let us get our runs on the board. Let them do the worrying and the calculating.

Poor Phil Slocombe fell first ball to Norbert Phillip. A mixed blessing for Essex this, for it brought Vivian Richards to the crease with plenty of time at his disposal. Viv was in devastating form and could be quite impossible to bowl to. On song he appeared able to drive any ball back over the bowler's head or to hook it past square leg, as he chose. He was the main threat to Essex, though if they could dismiss him early their spirits would rise. Playing with Viv releases pressure, yet if he fails, the opposition feel that they have the initiative and their confidence rises dramatically.

Rose struggled to find form, a captain carrying a heavy burden of responsibility. Richards almost immediately mistimed a Lever out-swinger and edged to McEwan at slip. A reliable poucher, McEwan missed the chance, a terrible moment for him. Then Rose edged tentatively and McEwan dropped another catch. Despite this let-off Rose continued to be at sea, unsure whether to battle on or to try to hit his way out of trouble. He played five successive maidens from Stuart Turner, afraid to unleash his fierce drives. It scarcely mattered, though, for Richards had decided it was his day and cut loose. He drove Lever through mid-wicket from outside off stump in disdainful manner. Lever folded his arms, stunned by the injustice of it all.

Rose tried to break his chains, just clearing mid-off with a mis-hit. An over later his harassed contribution ended, caught by East in the outfield. 86 for 2 in 26 overs. I joined Richards. He nodded an 'All right, man?' Apart from the odd 'Keep going, man' or 'Well played, Roeby' he doesn't say much at the wicket, preferring to encourage by his towering example.

He was in an uninhibited mood. As I struggled to gather momentum Richards raised the tone of the innings by launching into Keith Pont. By brute force he cracked Pont over mid-on. I advised him to 'cool it', but the next ball flashed over cover and the next was hit violently over the bowler's head. Not a bad ball amongst them. Viv had his head, no point in restraint.

Essex were in trouble. Taunton's boundaries are short and fast, and if the batsmen are on top runs can tumble upon each other. If Fletcher tried to prevent singles, boundaries might mount. If he patrolled the ropes, ones and twos could be snatched from accurate bowling, bringing six an over. In the first round Somerset had chased Warwickshire's 292 in 60 overs and reached it with time to spare. Runs are very hard to contain at Taunton, though Fletcher at least knew that Essex had batsmen capable of matching Somerset stroke for stroke.

Richards, remarkably relaxed for a semi-final, continued in extravagant vein. He stepped yards outside his leg stump to carve Ray East over extra cover for six. It was an outrageous liberty, a benefit-match shot. But it was that sort of a match as brilliance heaped upon brilliance. Viv reached his century, raising his arms Boycott-fashion to acknowledge the cheers. Not one of his great innings, it lacked his controlled mastery, but it was an extraordinary, flamboyant effort. His end was worthy, too: magnificently caught at mid-wicket by Mike Denness as he drove furiously.

Botham replaced Richards. He had 18 overs to develop his full repertoire of shots. Yet he was drawn to his doom as surely as Robin Hood was drawn by the Silver Arrow contest. He had to show that he could match Viv's blistering power and genius. East bowled a very slow lob. Botham duly stepped away to crack it over extra cover. Instead he missed the ball and it gently, almost apologetically, dislodged a bail. Utterly undismayed, Botham looked to the heavens before departing shaking his head. East had known that Ian never could resist a challenge, and the rest had been inevitable.

We did not suffer from Botham's wild stroke. Vic Marks immediately struck form. No batsmen in the game, once Rose had gone, struggled to score runs. My dismissal brought in Dennis Breakwell and he, too, discovered dazzling form so that after Richards' fall over 100 runs were scored in 17 overs.

287 was a formidable total, especially in a supposedly tight semi-final. Surely Essex could not chase so many, not against Garner and Botham. Somerset players, officials and supporters were very confident.

Denness was quickly snapped up by Marks at mid-wicket. Apart from McEwan's misses, not a chance went begging all day. McEwan joined Gooch, as threatening a combination as Richards and Botham. McEwan bore a heavy burden, having dropped Richards. Like most men brought up on hard, true pitches, McEwan hits hard and straight through the line of the ball. He is particularly severe on spinners, though he avows an inability to cope with flight and guile. So he clobbers them. Gullible lot, the Poms!

McEwan was soon driving from a high back-lift and cutting Garner behind point, another fast-wicket stroke. Rose was forced to rest Garner and Botham: he might need a burst from each later. Our spearhead had not achieved a decisive breakthrough, nor had they been able to pin down high-class batsmen on this pitch. Burgess and Dredge tried to stem the flow of runs. If Essex had fallen behind the clock, risks would have been necessary and vital wickets might have resulted. Suddenly, with things going well, McEwan drove loosely at Burgess's inswinger and lost his off stump. Would Essex falter at last?

Fletcher, Essex captain and a tough competitor despite the frail, gnomish appearance, was in next. He is well used to run chases and has developed a technique for scoring quickly by manoeuvring his feet, disturbing the bowler's line and length. He is capable of pacing an innings, of disrupting a field without hitting powerfully or in the air.

Gooch plundered on, giving Fletcher valuable overs to settle. Breakwell twisted his ankle in the field as, ever a bag of nerves, he turned to scamper after a ball. Rose found himself a bowler short. He had to find someone to bowl Breakwell's overs. He tried Marks for the final over before tea. Marks bowled poorly, appearing terribly weary, and the experiment cost 13 runs. At tea Essex stood at 114 for 2 in 25 overs. It was a superb response, a fighting display. We had been 80 for 2 at the same stage. We realised that semi-finals had to be won. However strong your position, you could not release the pressure for an instant. 174 needed in 35 overs, a distinct possibility. Rose knew that Richards must bowl those spare overs. In a tight corner it is so often to Richards that we turn. He is highly competitive, is committed to victory and has a stature that almost demands responsibility. He has been known to snatch the ball off reluctant bowlers in big games.

Reluctantly Rose introduced Garner after tea, as he desperately strove for a breakthrough. It was a move he had to make, though it reduced Garner's influence in the final overs. Garner tried a leg-cutter, Gooch was good enough to touch it and walked as Taylor held up the catch. Now, for Christ's sake, Essex must fade.

Hardie was next in, a gutsy, effective batsman. Startlingly he, too, immediately played with aggressive fluency. Richards bowled tidily but Essex motored on with controlled hitting, with batting of experience and quality. Fletcher nibbled along, varying the direction and pace of his strokes. He drove fiercely into gaps or rolled the ball to deep fielders, scrambling a second run that would have been unavailable had he hit the ball harder.

Hardie's breezy effort ended as he risked an extra run to Slocombe, who threw down the stumps with Hardie inches short. This was Slocombe's contribution to the game, a game in which every participant played some vital part. With every wicket the crowds roared, singing their songs of 'Rosey's Army' and 'Cider Drinking'.

Pont was next in. A cheerful extrovert, he defied the tension and launched into Richards, striking two massive blows into St James' church. But Viv's overs were nearly finished, he'd escaped lightly. Botham returned, determined to have some impact on a game that had so far passed him by. He bowled to Pont who hooked it high to me at long leg. Ages to study it, to reflect upon the consequences of dropping it. I hung on, and with unsuppressed delight tossed it into the air. Pont made as if to leave the field. Derek Taylor yelled at me. A no-ball! Pont could easily have run! And if he had . . . Bedlam!

Essex needed 52 in 8 overs. Pont rushed for a second to Botham at third man. The throw hurtled into Taylor's gloves with Pont feet adrift. With that lightning pick-up and throw, Botham's contribution was just starting. Botham to Fletcher, who drove uppishly. Botham caught the ball in his stomach and hurled it triumphantly to the skies. Fletcher hung his head in disappointment, flung his bat into the air. He had conceived victory with his shrewd, tenacious innings: was it to be a mirage after all?

Phillip joined Turner. The very next ball Turner drove, Marks fielded, Phillip was sent back and Marks hit the one stump he could see. Again the tide had turned, surely for the final time. Suddenly Turner swung at Botham, skimming two balls to the fence. Another twist, and Essex had the edge. 23 needed in 3 overs with Garner, Botham and Dredge to bowl.

Botham's over was tidy, until Taylor somehow or other contrived to miss a take and the ball raced to the boundary. An extraordinary mishap. Turner tried another wild hit but missed and he was gone.

East and Smith together. East is a bit mad, liable to do anything. We'd much rather have had a sane, predictable individual at the centre of things.

Garner's final over was mean, and 13 were needed as Dredge of Frome stepped up to deliver the final six balls. Very raw and very tired was Colin. All of his enormous family were behind his arm as he offered a little prayer before running in to bowl.

The first bowl brought a single. Then East swished at a wide ball and edged it for four. A bad delivery. Essex were back in with a chance.

East swung again next ball, missed it and was bowled. Prodigious cheers. Our game. Then, horror of horrors, Dredge bowled his first no-ball of the season. Not only that, he tore after the defensive push and overthrew the ball so that Lever scrambled three.

Four needed from two balls. Anyone's game. Just pray the ball does not come to you; imagine being responsible for losing.

A single off the penultimate delivery left Lever needing three off the last to win. Or so it emerged after lengthy discussions that prolonged the agony and heightened the drama.

Lever swung lustily. The ball flew off the edge towards Rose at deep point. Rose did not pick up the ball against the surging background, not for a horrifying instant at any rate. Taylor screamed for the ball. Rose hurled it first bounce, a yard off-target. Taylor picked it up well and dived at the wickets just as Smith flung himself to complete the winning run. Umpire Jepson held up his finger, Botham and Dredge jumped to the heavens, the crowd charged onto the pitch, the players rushed from it. Smith trudged disconsolately to his utterly silent dressing room, to make the long journey home along the M4.

We searched for some peace and quiet to unwind, hiding in a back room away from the shouts of relief and the taste of champagne. Victory and defeat had been so very close, yet were so absolutely different. We were to discover that three weeks later.

SOMERSET

B. C. Rose	c East b Pont	24
P. A. Slocombe	lbw Phillip	0
I. V. A. Richards	c Denness b Gooch	116
P. M. Roebuck	c Lever b Phillip	57
I. T. Botham	b East	7
V. J. Marks	not out	33
G. I. Burgess	b Lever	5
D. Breakwell	not out	17
Extras		28
Total (6 wkts, 60 overs)		287

Did not bat: D. J. S. Taylor, J. Garner, C. H. Dredge.
Fall of wickets: 1–2, 2–86, 3–189, 4–208, 5–247, 6–255.
Bowling: Lever 12–0–61–1; Phillip 11–1–56–2; Turner 8–6–22–0; Pont 6–1–35–1; Gooch 12–0–42–1; East 11–1–43–1.

ESSEX

M. H. Denness	c Marks b Dredge	3
G. A. Gooch	c Taylor b Garner	61
K. S. McEwan	b Burgess	37
K. W. R. Fletcher	c & b Botham	67
B. R. Hardie	run out	21
K. R. Pont	run out	39
N. Phillip	run out	1
S. Turner	b Botham	12
R. E. East	b Dredge	10
N. Smith	run out	6
J. K. Lever	not out	5
Extras		25
Total (60 overs)		287

Fall of wickets: 1–9, 2–70, 3–127, 4–166, 5–246, 6–248, 7–248, 8–266, 9–281.
Bowling: Garner 12–1–46–1; Dredge 12–0–60–2; Botham 12–1–48–2; Burgess 12–1–43–1; Breakwell 2–0–11–0; Marks 1–0–13–0; Richards 9–1–41–0.
Somerset won by losing fewer wickets.

11

Fletch

Most captains are ruthless in their first seasons, as determination to win thrusts less immediate values into the back of the mind and beyond. After all, if you have no fire early on, how can you assert yourself thereafter? Joan of Arc had the right idea, full of passion and fury, concerned with victory and not with bonus points or bringing on the younger soldiers. Brian Rose and John Barclay, in 1978 and 1981 respectively, had an unsuspected ability to turn a Nelsonian eye or Van Goghian ear to activities that were far from prudish.

Most of these firebrands mellow as the years take their toll. Some mellow more slowly than others (Brian Close scarcely mellowed at all!), but a certain reticence, a withdrawal from the early stark attitudes, is usually detectable within a couple of years. If success has blessed his reign, or if it is seen to be beyond possibility even if Martin Bormann's view of things is adopted, the leader will retreat a little, content for events to unfold as they will. Wise captains learn, with Canute, that the tide of affairs cannot long be resisted. Even Brearley could not prevent Warwickshire chasing 216 in 40 overs in 1980, for 1980 was Warwickshire's year, when in the John Player League they were irresistible.

Of current county captains only two retain their devotion to victory, only two still pursue success with zealous enthusiasm: Mike Brearley and Keith Fletcher.

Brearley, ever the rationaliser, leads Middlesex as he led England, with cunning and zeal. He uses every available weapon to its fullest, including a cutting tongue. He senses the weaknesses of opponents very quickly, knows by instinct which bowlers they least want to face, which unusual field-placements might unsettle them. Brearley enjoys teasing opponents, testing their nerve. When Somerset played

Middlesex last season he stood in the middle of the pitch three yards in front of me, calling to ask of his bowler whether he required any off-side fielders for so leg-side a player as Roebuck. Undaunted by these withering comments, I advised Brearley that he most certainly did not need a mid-off, and suggested that he should add another slip as I was bound to edge one in a minute. It was around this time that the cover point, one Jeff Thomson, sent for a deck chair as he felt redundant, too!

Michael Brearley is a sharp captain, who moves his men with the intellectual incisiveness of a chess player. Keith Fletcher's approach is more simply defined. He wants to win, very badly. Fletcher, the gnome by appearance but 'Fletch' by name, is a hardy cricketer, a survivor as adept in his field as his namesake doing 'porridge' in Slade Prison is in his. His years as captain of Essex, long-suffering years, have taught him to keep his head low and not to raise his hopes too high. As a captain he is a grafter who nags away at his job from April to September. He works hard, digging his heels in if the winds are rough, undeterred by setbacks.

He is a rigorous, tough captain, too. That frail appearance is deceptive, a cloak disguising a strong will. The pottering gait and shuffling feet, the tangled pads and the quizzical air create an impression of a quiet, mystical leader, a Napoleon of cricket. It is all nonsense! Fletcher is far from meek, he is a thoroughly professional, fighting captain. He asks nothing and gives less.

Nor is he over-sympathetic to the misfortunes of opponents. When Pakistan were caught on a Headingley wicket saturated by water mysteriously ignorant of covers they escaped with a draw, saved by another torrential downpour. Everyone was relieved, embarrassed that a Test match could so easily have been decided by such ill-luck. Well, nearly everyone that is. John Arlott expressed this view to the gnome, who replied that he'd be happy to win in any circumstances. After all, he'd experienced Pakistani umpires and Pakistani wickets and saw no need to be kind or generous. If the dice fell his way, tough luck. No, Fletcher's opponents need not expect much sympathy. He is not a man given to showing emotion himself, having borne the slings of Essex's near-misses throughout the 1970s with dignified fortitude; a shake of the head and a dry comment sufficed to express disappointment. Or perhaps it is just that the extroverts around him drive him

into his shell just as, so I hear, managers of can-can troupes withdraw
into nervous silence.

If Keith Fletcher is a hard, unrelenting skipper it is scarcely
surprising. Cricket has dealt him some fierce blows. His Test debut at
Headingley, as replacement for local slip specialist Phil Sharpe, was
dogged by dropped catches and cruel gibes. It was an experience unlikely to foster liberal attitudes. Those harsh days, and the apparently
unending series of disasters with Essex, ensured that the quiet man
developed into a fiercely competitive leader, utterly determined to
overcome all adversity. His county team play their cricket with the
aggressive instincts of Australians, as failure drives them even harder
towards triumph. When at last they took the Benson and Hedges Cup
in 1979, it was fitting reward for an unforgiving, persistent team led
with dedicated shrewdness.

With this cool ruthlessness Keith Fletcher remains very much in
charge of his team. He may look as if he could not bring himself to say
boo to a pheasant, but he has an undoubted authority which does not
need proud flourish or forceful statements. At a recent team meeting,
convened to discuss various changes to a faltering batting line-up,
Fletcher sat impassive as the debate ranged from the whimsical to the
outrageous. Suddenly he rose, announced, 'I'm batting at 4, sort the
rest out yourselves' and promptly left the room! Nothing much
changed.

Most of Keith Fletcher's comments are pithy and show his dry wit.
He surveys the harshness of cricket with a wry, sometimes terse sense
of humour. He is not one for the hearty guffaw, defiant of fate's
sinuous twists. He appreciates the little things that flicker across the
scene, only observed by those with a keen eye. His comments, if
something does slip out, usually stick in the mind – like Mona Lisa's
smile they have a sardonic, enigmatic quality. Last season, in the
Essex v. Somerset match, the umpiring was a little unusual. After a
particularly astonishing decision, the gnome nodded his head and said
out of the corner of his mouth in a high-pitched cockney voice, ''Ere,
Rupert, you've got to hit the ball to be lbw in this game. If you miss it
you can only be caught!' We chuckled, and it was some time before I
realised that he had called me Rupert, which is not quite my name.
No-one had ever called me that before. Several Essex players heard
the remark too, and were similarly confused. It emerged that, though

I'd been playing against Essex for six years, Fletcher thought my name to be Rupert Roebuck and had addressed me accordingly. It has been, ever since.

And Fletcher appreciated John Edrich's comment to him as he pottered in to bat in the first Test of the 1974–75 tour. As Lillee and Thomson strained for Pommy victims, Fletcher enquired of Edrich as to the nature of things in the middle. 'One tour too many, Fletch, one tour too many,' sighed Edrich. That succinct statement appealed to Fletcher's battle-hardened, if not battle-scarred view of the world. No doubt he chuckled a wry chuckle before jumping around his stumps in that deceptively timid way.

Probably he needs this understated humour to persevere through thin times. An avid gardener, every winter he yearns to return to his garden, hoping to pass his time with spade and secateurs. Often his best hopes are thwarted, as he is invited to tour here or there. One winter, just as he was sharpening his pruning shears, he felt a looming giant towering over him. It was mighty Tony Greig, no less. Greig asked after Fletcher's winter plans. 'Oh, a bit of gardening and a pint or two in the local, Greiggy. I'm really looking forward to it.' 'Sorry, Fletch,' replied the England captain, 'you're coming to Calcutta with me.' It was not entirely clear whether Keith Fletcher received this news with overwhelming delight.

Naturally, there is more to Fletcher's survival than tending roses and subdued smiles. He is also a very fine batsman. He has scored consistently well in county cricket for 15 years, with a technique that is sound, unspectacular and highly effective. He tucks the ball off his pads with a late twirl of the wrists, and can crash the ball square on the off-side with surprising force. His style is grooved to late adjustments, to nibbling the ball into gaps that were there 15 years ago and still cannot be filled. He is a pragmatic batsman, who accumulates runs just as he always has, by intelligent use of his feet and by careful placement. If a field is set deep, he'll not waste energy smiting the ball, he'll stroke it into a gap and try to scamper a second. He knows he lacks Gooch's resounding power and McEwan's majesty, but experience has taught him how to score every bit as quickly, almost without being noticed. Often Fletcher is 35 before anyone realises he has reached 10.

He is, too, a superb architect of a one-day innings. Again he scores quickly, without hitting straight sixes or the like. He'll upset bowlers by shuffling his feet, by feigning to go this way or that. He'll skip away from his stumps to crack straight balls past point. Like Alan Knott in his prime, Fletcher can be very hard to bowl to in this mood. He knows exactly what risks are worth taking, and when, and is also a skilful timer of a chase, Essex's best. He frets away at the bowler, disrupting him, annoying him. With Fletcher at the helm, Essex appear to be in control. In the famous Somerset v. Essex Gillette Cup semi-final in 1978, recounted in the previous chapter, it was Fletcher who bore the burden of the chase. Fletcher reduced the target notch by notch, sticking at his job with the perseverance of an ant. When his team lost on a technicality, it must have seemed as if Essex would never win a trophy.

As it turned out, it was merely another bitter setback, another sad blow to be survived. Fletcher has survived many twists of fortune and has not keeled over in despair. He is more robust than he appears, maybe not a dynamic cricketer but a dogged and cussedly effective one.

12

My Only Cricket Riot

Most cricketers have their riots in Karachi, Delhi or Jamaica. My riot took place in Corfu, just off the west coast of Greece.

I'd played cricket several times in Greece. I holiday there after every English cricket season and invariably end up playing somewhere for someone. In Athens we played on a dirt soccer pitch with a mat laid down in the middle of it. No effort was made to flatten the dirt; after all, the mat was flat! I was playing for a team raised by eccentric ex-Somerset captain R. J. O. Meyer (see Chapter 9). We were to play British Airways. Somerset bowler, Colin Dredge, was in our team (he was unimpressed by the Acropolis – 'Didn't think much of it. Couldn't live there, could you?') and bowled the first ball. It pitched on a good length, lifted and carried on lifting for some time as the slips and wicket-keeper watched it. It kept rising ever upward, eventually reaching the distant boundary second bounce. If that was his loosener . . ., we all thought. Colin was advised to bowl slow half-volleys. Needless to say, he was belted all around the ground.

Matting wickets can offer prodigious bounce. This prevents tall bowlers from hitting the stumps. Most Greek bowlers employ 'curly' actions, bowling from about shoulder height, threatening to clip the umpire's ear. They skim the ball down, hoping it will skid. This gives them the chance of clean bowling someone or appealing for lbw, and with Greek umpires it's not wise to be struck anywhere below the ribs!

Corfu is not quite as primitive as Athens. The square has a concrete strip in the middle, which ensures an even, bouncy wicket. The boundaries vary: on one side are the cafés and tavernas which attract the players and tourists with shade and Greek coffee. On the far side is a short grass boundary with a large car park behind it. The furthest edge of the car park is the boundary unless the ball hits a car or coach on its way, in which case four is signalled. Let me now introduce you to a favourite Corfiote tactic. When you bat there is not a car or coach to be seen and the boundaries are gigantic. During the interval (it couldn't be called Tea, for there is no tea, and 'Capuccino' doesn't sound quite right), by mysterious magic the car park gradually fills until as you take the field it is full and the boundary 30 yards shorter! Incidentally this car park ploy works in reverse if the Corfiotes bat first. W. G. Grace would have been proud of it!

If the Corfiotes do field second, another tactic is available. No, not to ply the batsmen with ouzo or retsina – that's taken for granted – but slow over-rates. Night falls very quickly in those parts, so if you place the field with care and change it as often as possible, it can be dark just as the opposition are nearing your total.

They are not as naive as they pretend, these Corfiotes. After all, the Greeks produced Platonic philosophy, the Parthenon and Melbourne. Of course, all they really care about nowadays is politics and soccer. If an election is taking place in Athens, 600,000 people will meet in Sintagna square on three successive nights for three different parties. And if they shout 'one' or 'two' it is not a call to run, it is delight at the fortunes of AEK, Olympiakos or Panathenaikos. By the way, the Greeks developed their language especially so as to confuse the English. 'OK' means 'no', 'nay' means 'yes'. We English tend to regard that sort of behaviour as Irish. Somerset players have been known to attempt similar things in benefit games, 'yes' meaning 'no', and 'no' 'yes'. The time to worry in that case is when your partner mutters 'slow down' as you pass!

Now, this riot. We were on our second trip to Corfu, having a terrific time. The previous year an individual named Pandreus had slaughtered our attack to score 126 in 20 overs, hitting some mighty blows over the hotels and tavernas. This time we were determined to beat Phaiax and Gymnasticos. Well, we beat Phaiax, notwithstanding cars, umpires, ouzo and donkeys wandering across the pitch with a perplexed air. For the Gymnasticos game we decided to infiltrate one of our own umpires, to even things up a bit.

They batted first, scoring 128 in 30 overs. Our openers, the usual sacrificial lambs, set about the chase. In the third over one of our men may (or may not) have tickled the ball to the 'keeper: 'just a faint one,' as the pros say. Now there is no rubbish about walking in Corfu: if they appeal you stand there looking indignant, rub your elbow and wave your arms about (not easy to do at the same time!). If this does not work, you mutter dark words and leave the field shaking your head.

Our man edged the ball, or missed it, and our hero in a white coat said 'not out', or 'OK out' as the Greeks put it. The bowler, a fierce Heathcliff type, grunted and bowled again. Our man swept him past square leg for four. That was a mistake, for the bowler went berserk. He grabbed a stump and chased our umpire around the field. This caused a certain amount of surprise. After a while the batsmen decided to help the umpire in distress. Thereupon the opposition, espying that the odds had now swung in favour of the visitors, joined in the mêlée. At about this time, those of us awaiting our turn at the crease rushed into the fray waving cricket bats, newspapers or Grecian urns.

The growing crowd enjoyed this spectacle enormously. 'Better than Spartacus,' someone exclaimed. Several American tourists thought it a substantial improvement on the cricket, though a couple of them assumed it was a natural part of the game. Maybe they'd seen Gaelic football in Dublin, which makes most riots look like peace marches. Of course the locals joined in, even Stan Bradley from Bolton joined in. (Stan was visiting Corfu trying to arrange a Brass Band Festival there. An optimist, Stan.) For a while it resembled a punch-up at the OK Corral, one of those where John Wayne is clobbering everyone before James Stewart stops the fight and puts everyone except John Wayne in jail.

I suppose it lasted in all about five minutes. For a while it was a bit tense, but a few ouzos restored international relations. Or perhaps it was Panathenaikos' victory which cheered everyone up. And I fancy the American tourists were right – the riot was much more fun than the cricket!

13

Something Fell From Heaven

Gradually the ball descended, obeying Newton's law. No snow on it, for the day was warm. The batsman waited and watched. Eventually he smote at it vigorously, with all the might he could muster. But he was deceived; the ball had not yet arrived. As he completed his lusty swing, the ball bounced and trickled towards the stumps. A bail was dislodged before the agonised batsman could retrieve his dignity. Another victim for Teer, another fool rushing in. As the disconsolate batsman trudged to the pavilion he muttered under his breath (as Agatha Christie victims mutter mysterious dying words), 'Something fell from heaven.'

Norman Teer bowls donkey-drops. He's been at it a long time, and with considerable success. He launches the ball far into the skies and then relaxes, awaiting the outcome. Something usually happens. His proud boast is to be 'the highest bowler in Somerset', though he concedes that Joel Garner is the tallest. His deliveries, sent into orbit from 24 yards, after a brief skip or two, soar at least 15 feet into the air. Once in a while he slips in a quicker ball which rises to only twice the height of man. In Gambia his deliveries often bounced over the batsman's head. Horrified Gambians were dumbfounded by this yo-yo style of bowling, and fell in droves. When it bounces, if it bounces, his donkey-drop will spin a little. That's an unnecessary touch. Probably Nureyev could sing, too, but who needs it?

From this you may gather that Norman Teer is an original, a remnant from more generous cricketing days. Every ball is a challenge, miserly efforts at run-saving are ignored. It's wickets that matter. Once in a while, say in a 30-over game, Norman's figures of five overs, three for 53, appear a bit of a luxury. But then, like most bowlers of his kind, Norman is captain, selector and organiser of his club, the Mendip Acorns. In these roles he usually manages to conclude that he should bowl, if not all the time, at least a good deal of it. He took well over 100 wickets in 1980, including several bags of '7 for' and '6 for'. One does not ask '7 for what?' or '6 for what?'

With these numerous wickets, a northern dialect, a balding patch and an air of immensely serious intent, one might imagine that Norman's deliveries contain a measure of guile, a touch or two of the wisdom gathered over the years by this sprightly 65-year-old. Not so. Norman is beyond wisdom. His philosophy is simple. 'They can't resist 'em, y'know,' he confides to uninitiated team-mates. And they can't. Norman arrives at the crease, orders his troops to disappear in various directions (mostly leading to the leg-side boundary) and measures his skip. Up floats the ball. Each delivery is a potential incident. A six, a four, a brilliant stop or a wicket. 'Dots' are few and far between. Maidens come about once a year (I'm told the position is similar in Cardiff).

At Paulton, in a match reduced to 12 overs, things were going badly. The ball was wet and no-one could grip it. Zaheer was playing for the Acorns. He had a bowl but his over cost him 12 runs. So Norman came on into the wind. Norman hates bowling into the face of even a gentle breeze. His first ball climbed as high as usual. The batsman advanced to dispatch it. He swung the bat but missed the ball. It rolled slowly towards the stumps. Recovering his wits, the batsman rushed back to his crease and put his foot behind the barely moving ball. Norman, ever keen for wickets, appealed for lbw. The umpire ruled in his favour. The batsman was stunned, shouting down the pitch, 'The ruddy ball wouldn't even have reached the ruddy wicket!' But he went his weary way in the end.

Things do happen when Norman is bowling. On another famous occasion, this time in Tavistock, Norman was being hit to the leg-side boundary rather frequently by an aggressive left-hander. Norman thereupon sent all his fieldsmen to the affected area (as sandbags are sent to help stem floods). The left-hander, espying the field, shrewdly decided to drive the ball to the cover boundary. He succeeded only in destroying his stumps, sending pieces of wood flying in all directions. Once again fielders fell about in helpless mirth as a furious batsman retraced his steps, trying to think of a convincing story to tell his captain.

If these incidents suggest that Norman Teer plays in a low standard of cricket, they are misleading: the Mendip Acorns have included Zaheer, Underwood, Vivian Richards and Don Shepherd amongst their numbers. But to resist Norman's bait is not merely a matter of ability; it requires humility. It is the devil tempting Jesus on the hill. Pride demands that he must be hit for six, for how can one be a man and yet collect gentle singles off these skyscrapers? No, no red-blooded man could resist the challenge. Let the voice of caution be still awhile, let the boundary fielders be alert. Alas, the boundary is well staffed, and it is not so easy to hit such slow balls for six. And so numerous self-respecting batsmen succumb, falling into the trap as knowingly as lemmings fall into the sea.

Norman derives enormous pleasure from watching opponents fall prey to his wiles. He loves his cricket in all its variations; the more improbable the venue, the more outlandish the game, the better. He has organised many overseas tours for his club, 25 in the past 12 years. Sierra Leone, the West Indies, Malta and the Far East have all been visited – not bad for an apparently innocuous tyre salesman.

That frail, *Diary of a Nobody* appearance is deceptive. Norman is a talented organiser. His tourists have included opera singers, academics, bookmakers and mechanics. The tyre business is a side-show, an excuse to spend a day by the phone arranging another tour. His only concession to the exigencies of business is to encourage Acorns to buy Teer's tyres (Teer's tyre pressure, it is called), just as Al Capone encouraged clients to buy his liquor. Nor is Norman as shy as he looks. Startled Acorns often emerge from a 'plane to be greeted by dignitaries, steel bands and dancing girls. In Barbados, Dr Eric Glair, by all accounts a formidable man, met the Acorns. ''Morning, Eric,' ventured our intrepid leader. Mr Teer has the hide of a hippo and the nerve of an unhelmeted batsman. He needs it, to bowl like that.

Acorns' cricket is deadly serious, particularly on tour. Humour arises from a haphazard series of events, from an improbable combination of individuals (for Acorns' teams include examples of all shapes, hues, ages and abilities). It is not forced, the cricket is not for fun. Often the humour is unconscious. There is nothing necessarily funny about Norman Teer and Derek Underwood bowling in harness. Yet in the West Indies in 1971 they were a hugely popular pairing. Quite what Deadly Derek made of it all one can only speculate. It was not long before local radio stations were providing running descriptions of the game, with commentators in danger of falling from their lofty perches as hilarity increased. By the end of the tour people were coming from miles around to study this extraordinary bowler. Norman was a hero. Not that he was impressed in the slightest by all this fuss. He wheeled away with a lot of flight and a bit of guile, watching with a perplexed air as the ball soared over the boundary, or explaining the subtleties of each wicket with the aplomb of Trueman in his prime.

For all the cheerful optimism of his bowling, Norman is immensely competitive. Woe betide any fielder who misses a chance of his bowling. Any ball hit in the air brings forth the view that the nearest beggar should have caught it. Possibly Norman does not select enough beggars. Once, amidst the usual tirade of hooks, cuts, drives and sweeps, a batsman popped up a ball into the vacant short-leg position. Captain Teer sidled up to me at the completion of the over and said, 'I knew I should have put someone there.' Volunteers for the forward short-leg position to Norman Teer might have been few and far between in a team of VCs, I suspect.

As a cricketer Norman is, you may agree, colourful and imaginative. He is also not beyond a little deviousness. It is darkly whispered that Acorns teams are chosen so as to include plenty of batting and a scarcity of bowling. As the team gathers, Norman (the man who selected the team) sometimes peers around his players and discovers, to his apparent dismay, that he has no opening bowlers. 'Better open up myself,' he concludes. Once this ploy worked well. Bowling the first over to a proficient batsman, Norman sent all his fielders to the boundary and served up a juicy, slow long hop. The opener duly smote it fiercely back to the bowler. It landed in our hero's stomach, knocking him to the ground. He clung to the ball, rising in triumph as he dusted himself, to explain, 'I knew he'd do that.'

Despite all the batsmen in his team, Norman often discovers, to his evident astonishment, that 'though our batting is strong, we don't appear to have a second opener'. Whereupon he straps on his pads and cuts and carves successfully until Cyril or Archie, well used to Teer's way, judge their President to be lbw.

Despite advancing years, I expect Norman will continue for a long

1. Somerset's new pavilion – a reflection of the bubbling enthusiasm for cricket in the South-West. (*E-Pix*)

2. Someone, somewhere must have a picture of Ian Botham playing a defensive shot. (*E-Pix*)

3. Viv Richards displaying all his majestic, explosive power. Just look at the battered middle of the bat! (*E-Pix*)

4. Viv and Ian – fierce friends and rivals – with Ian's son, Liam. The sight of them all late-night shopping together in Sainsbury's on one occasion is still talked about in Taunton. (*Peter McCombe*)

5. 'Trout': a high arm and a grimace. It's hard to take him quite so seriously after the games between Mr Roebuck's XI and Mr Barclay's XI – see Chapter 6. (*Patrick Eagar*)

6. Vic Marks sends down one of his slow off-breaks with the expression on his face which he usually reserves for my driving – see Chapter 8. (*E-Pix*)

7. The 'Old Blighter', as ever resolutely on the front foot, and no doubt inspiring his partner by his immense determination. (*Patrick Eagar*)

8. No wonder Barbadians are so strong on the leg side: you get six if you hit the ball into the sea. (*Patrick Eagar*)

9. Night cricket is a magnificent spectacle, but in England (this is Stamford Bridge) it is usually either cold or wet and is unlikely to catch on. Why not a 'twilight league' in July and August? (*Patrick Eagar*)

10. 'Big Bird' flapping another one down. (*E-Pix*)

11. Brian Rose (with specs). He leans back as he wallops a straight drive, yet he usually keeps the ball down. (*E-Pix*)

12. Lord's, 1979 – victory at last. It tasted all the better after the years of disappointment. (*Peter McCombe*)

13. Just to prove that even so leg-side a player as Roebuck can essay an off-drive! (*E-Pix*)

while. 'Just one more tour,' he repeats from time to time, much as Frank Sinatra would say, 'Just one more concert.' Anyhow, he still has one ambition left: to travel to a game on a camel. The Acorns are presently planning a tour to Bahrain. Watch this space.

14

Somerset v. Essex

1978 Sunday League

The previous day, the day of the 1978 Gillette Cup Final, had been a bitter disappointment. After chasing 297 against Warwickshire in the first round, scoring 330 at Cardiff, defeating Kent in a tense quarter-final and scraping home in the epic semi-final with Essex, we were favourites at Lord's. We had fought tooth and nail all season, every ball of every day. We were a young team with a new captain in a club which had never tasted success, a club with an air of inferiority, country cousins easily downtrodden by powerful teams from the East and from the North.

But things were different now. We had Ian Botham and Viv Richards, Brian Rose and Joel Garner. Teams no longer looked forward to playing us. We'd enjoyed a highly successful season, and victory at Lord's would have been a fitting climax. Everything had gone wrong. The champagne was never opened. We'd played like an emotionally bankrupt team, a team with nothing more to give. A team trying too hard to win.

Travelling back to Taunton alone had provided plenty of time for morose reflection, listening to Christopher Martin-Jenkins describing our poor performance. Surely to goodness we couldn't throw away our last hope as well? This was the final day of a long season. We only needed to beat Essex to seize our first trophy. If we lost and Hampshire beat Middlesex . . .

It would be Essex! Bitter rivals of Somerset, their history, like Somerset's, indicates a strange, unpredictable genius. A persistent failure to achieve seemed inevitable, with the occasional, inspired, apparently impossible triumph to spice things up. Essex had never won a trophy either, and were grimly determined to deny us our hour.

Despite arriving home at midnight, I awoke fresh and full of mustard. When I arrived at the ground, it was humming with yet another massive crowd. Strangely, everyone felt much more lively, as if a load had been lifted by defeat the previous day. Possibly it was superficial, like those pre-war years of tinsel and jollity: cheerful defiance as overwhelming disaster inexorably approached.

As I changed, Brian Rose asked me if I wanted to play. I was as weary as anyone in our team, and had missed a few games through illness induced by tiredness. By 1979 we had learnt to prosper under pressure, hardened by the experiences of this harrowing season. Otherwise selection seemed straightforward. Phil Slocombe was preferred to Vic Marks, the rest held their places. Or at least so we assumed. It was only as we took the field, to rousing cheers, that we realised that Joel Garner was not playing. Hallam Moseley had bowled well all season and had been an integral part of our Sunday XI. He'd bowled very well in Garner's absence with Littleborough. Presumably Rose felt obliged to give Hallam his chance to win a medal. So Garner was omitted, a critical decision though a courageous one.

Hallam contributed a superb opening spell to launch the game, bowling his eight overs for 20 runs and the vital wicket of McEwan. We fielded very well, alert and accurate. The crowd were behind us, applauding anything remotely resembling success. Essex stumbled to 103 for 4 in 30 overs, not a strong position. They could only expect to score around 160, well within our capabilities.

Then, quite suddenly, everything fell apart. Our nerves had held so well, we'd escaped so often from the very dentures of defeat, that this decline was inexplicable.

In the thirty-first over Fletcher cut loose. He'd been dropped behind the wicket first ball and had bided his time since. In the space of a few balls Somerset's contained effort fell into pieces. Mistake tumbled upon mistake, misfields, overthrows, missed catches. Confusion reigned. Fletcher tore into Dredge and Botham, repeatedly stepping away to lash straight balls to the cover boundary. The crowd hushed, not knowing how to rescue their sinking team, wanting to restore confidence. The slaughter continued, with no Joel Garner to bring back to restore order. 190 Essex scored, far more than had been anticipated half an hour previously.

We slumped into chairs, the good spirits of the morning gone. We were white with effort and weariness. Roy Kerslake, our chairman, pointed out that 190 was well within our abilities, advising us to delete from memory those final, tumultuous overs. Mere reasoning, though, could not brighten the gloom.

Rose and Denning launched our innings. They had been an excellent opening pair in limited-over games, ever ready to dart swift singles. A fine combination of styles, too, with Rose's magnificent straight driving and Denning's cutting and carving. They failed at Lord's and they failed this day, too. I was strapping on my pads as the first groan rumbled. Next minute, as I searched for gloves, a tired Rose returned. Denning lasted only a little longer, and again everything rested on Richards.

Viv was batting under immense pressure. Well-meaning supporters had reminded him of his centuries in earlier rounds of the Gillette, suggesting that he was bound to score another in the final. Viv, a man deeply loyal to his team and desperate for Somerset to win, had contributed a tentative 41. Not too bad really! Yet everyone considered it a failure, particularly Viv. He was the same in this game, trying too hard, repressing his natural genius. Instead of regally disposing of the ball, he tried to guide it here, place it there. He was so different in 1979, in the World and Gillette Cup finals, sweeping to majestic hundreds in both games.

I joined this restrained Richards at 18 for 2. I'd played too cautiously at Lord's, and decided to open out here. It was so much easier for me to be bold, without the cares of the team on my shoulders. Things went well for half an hour, as I clobbered a few boundaries. Then Viv fell, tamely for him, clipping a soft catch to mid-wicket. He was furious. His pent-up frustration had found no outlet on the field. Botham entered the arena, determined to turn the game. We crawled back into the match until, just as the tide turned, a wicket fell. I tried to tickle East through slip, mis-read his arm ball and lost my off bail. I left the field, disappointed but not annoyed. At least I'd had the courage to go for my shots this time.

Only then did the tension of the game strike me. Everything was so utterly quiet off the field. Much harder to watch a game from the pavilion, unable to affect events: far easier to be actively involved in it. Poor Roy Kerslake, Peter McCombe and Doc Challacombe, our backroom boys. They must suffer these agonies day after day.

I could not possibly watch these death throes. I changed and went for a stroll around town. It was beautifully tranquil in the streets, with scarcely anyone about at all. A few swans wandered down the Tone, undisturbed by muffled roars from a few hundred yards away. Ducks paddled about. A few families pottered around on their Sunday outing, blissfully unaware of events at the County ground.

It was a lovely day. I'd not noticed before.

I bumped into an old friend. Why wasn't he at the cricket? Took the family, couldn't bear it, how do you players manage? We don't, I smiled, we just keep going, hoping for the best. We can't cope really, who could?

Repeated roars: catches, boundaries, misfields? I hurried back to the ground, hopes raised. 140 for 6. Still in trouble, if anything deeper trouble. Apparently Essex had been getting into a state, too, as they doggedly strove to deny us as we had denied them three weeks earlier.

I returned to the 'box' from which players watch the game. It was very quiet, without even the usual running commentary to accompany each ball. We edged tantalisingly closer to the required rate, only to shudder under another body blow. Burgess was superbly caught as twist followed twist.

Gradually the game slipped away. It was not a quick death, our cause was never quite hopeless. Someone improbable might strike a six to add one last twist of the knife. The whole ground was over-wrought. It was impossible not to be swallowed up by the tension.

Thirteen in one over to avert disaster. Every fielder round the boundary. A streaky snick needed, orthodox strokes could not bring the runs. Jennings and Moseley swished away, lifting their heads as they strove for contact. Essex fieldsmen ran 50 yards to back up a throw. Four needed off one ball. Jennings swung mightily, miscued and ran. Essex swarmed from all directions. Hard though they ran, our men had no chance. Essex jumped to the heavens, strangely delighted at having dashed our hopes.

We descended very slowly to the dressing room. Utter silence prevailed as the vanquished sank wretchedly into chairs or hid behind newspapers. Not a word was said, no recriminations, no callow effort to revive spirits. Only Viv Richards reacted with aggression. He stormed into the bathroom and smashed his bat against a wall. Others retreated into their shells, unwilling to give any indication of emotion.

Meanwhile our crowd outside, thousands of them, roared and sang happy songs. They called for the players. This heightened the sorrow, as players felt they had let down their good-hearted followers. Yet the cheers continued, and eventually we responded with a wave and a thank-you. Already our supporters understood that we had given pleasure to many, and should not be too disappointed merely because the final hurdles had proved insurmountable. So they sang and clapped for over an hour.

As evening drew on the players gradually changed and went their various ways. Most of the crowd dispersed too, to find solace in a pint. Only Viv, Ian, Roy Kerslake, Peter McCombe and I remained to turn over the ashes of the season. Viv had never felt so sad before. He felt as if one of his family had died. We chatted far into the night, bemused by defeat. Eventually we too went our separate ways, vowing never again to suffer such humiliation. Next time we would at least enjoy ourselves, we would attack and the hell with it.

Strangely, precisely the same circumstances developed in 1979 as we found ourselves fighting the self-same battles. This time we emerged triumphant, and the champagne flowed freely. It tasted sweet, very sweet after defeat had been understood in its fullest intensity.

	ESSEX		
A. W. Lilley	c Denning	b Burgess	13
G. A. Gooch	c Burgess	b Botham	7
K. S. McEwan	b Moseley		2
K. W. R. Fletcher	not out		76
K. R. Pont	b Dredge		35
B. R. Hardie	b Botham		38
Extras			19
Total (5 wkts, 40 overs)			190

Did not bat: N. Phillip, S. Turner, R. E. East, N. Smith, J. K. Lever.
Fall of wickets: 1–16, 2–25, 3–29, 4–92, 5–190.
Bowling: Botham 8–0–38–2; Moseley 8–0–20–1; Burgess 8–0–20–1; Jennings 8–0–38–0; Dredge 8–0–55–1.

72

Somerset v. Essex

B. C. Rose	b Lever	9
P. W. Denning	c Smith b Phillip	8
I. V. A. Richards	c Hardie b Gooch	26
P. M. Roebuck	b East	30
I. T. Botham	c McEwan b Phillip	45
P. A. Slocombe	b Lever	20
G. I. Burgess	c & b Turner	0
K. F. Jennings	not out	14
C. H. Dredge	b Lever	14
D. J. S. Taylor	run out	4
H. R. Moseley	run out	0
Extras		18
Total (40 overs)		188

Fall of wickets: 1–18, 2–18, 3–69, 4–87, 5–139, 6–140, 7–157, 8–177, 9–185.

Bowling: Lever 8–0–38–3; Phillip 8–0–35–2; Gooch 8–0–31–1; Turner 8–0–32–1; East 8–0–34–1.

Essex won by 2 runs.

15

Brian Close

Many colourful characters have adorned Somerset cricket. From Sammy Woods and Jack White to Bill Andrews and Arthur Wellard, from Bill Alley and Colin McCool to Close and Botham, Somerset has been enriched by provocative, unpredictable men. Brian Close, the 'bald old blighter' as Alan Gibson dubbed him, or 'the Godfather' as we called him, brought to Taunton a fierce individualism and an uncompromising will to win.

He came when his best cricketing days were behind him, when a topsy-turvy career was gradually coming to its end. Those last few seasons were as explosive, as turbulent as most of the others. Brian Close left cricket not with a whimper, but with a bang. He retired in 1977 still cursing, still gritting his teeth, still trying to belt balls over deep mid-wicket, still standing at short leg giggling and glaring. We missed him when he left and realised how much we had enjoyed his personality, for all its impulsiveness.

Brian Close left a fund of anecdotes in his wake. His total commitment and his originality ensured that life was never dull under his leadership. Close took chances as a captain and as a man. He did not put long leg at long leg, he moved him 17 feet in and a little wider than usual. You see, he'd had this vision of what was going to happen and he arranged his field accordingly. You'd find yourself fielding in no-man's land, wondering whether you ought to be a bit closer or just a touch deeper, feeling uneasy. But you'd stay put, just in case the Old Blighter was right. And you'd stay in exactly the correct place, having scraped a large mark in the ground to define your position. Then if there was a disaster, at least you could point feebly to your scrape. Alas, Close could move you around a touch here, a hint there, so you ended up with a series of crosses resembling a pools coupon.

But woe betide you if you strayed from your position, especially if truth enacted the vision. After an unusually ungenerous declaration, Close's victory drive was being easily thwarted by the Essex batsmen. Nevertheless he deployed his troops with minute attention to detail, fiercely clapping his hands at short leg at the merest hint of relaxation. As the players went through the final rites of a stalemated game, Hardie drove a skimming chance to Steve ('Aggro') Wilkinson at mid-on. Aggro had slipped a yard or two too deep, moved too late and muffed the chance. It did not seem to matter, and stumps were drawn a few overs later. Everyone left the field content. Not Close: he stormed into the dressing room muttering, 'If ——— Aggro had caught that ——— catch we'd have beaten the ———s.'

It was not in Close's nature to concede error easily. His best-laid plans were always being frustrated by someone's incompetence. His strength lay in the force of his convictions, the strength of his personality, not in his ability to doubt his own judgement. He led by drive and inspiration. Sometimes these inspirations succeeded, other times they fell in ruins. Against Gloucestershire in a Benson and Hedges game Close introduced Mervyn Kitchen and Richard Cooper into the attack. No-one quite knew why. Neither of these rotund characters had bowled in public for several seasons. Kitchen trapped Ron Nicholls with a wide long hop. Nicholls was furious! Then Cooper, who contrived to bowl no-balls off a three-pace amble, persuaded Procter to sky a high full toss (Aussies call 'em headhunters). Kitchen hovered under it awhile but sadly dropped the chance, amidst considerable swearing from short leg.

Richie Benaud, from the commentary box, hailed these manoeuvres as acts of genius. Nor did the drama end there. At lunch Close informed an already startled team that 'we're going to catch 'em unawares'. He proceeded to bowl out his best bowlers, leaving legspinners and medium-pacers to deliver the final 20 overs. Procter scored 150 and took 5 for 30, and Somerset lost by a mile. Yet how near success had been! Probably Brian Close's captaincy was more suited to the three-day game, which offers scope for flair and imagination, than to the essentially defensive limited-over matches in which gambles are usually luxuries.

Still, the Godfather was an extraordinary man, a mixture of King Lear storming in the wilderness and Churchill defying 'em on the beaches. An immensely strong man, too: as a youngster he used to sit in a sauna for half an hour (try it, at 100°), doing press-ups, burpees and the rest – now try that! He never doubted his own physical prowess. Watching an Ali v. Frazier fight, Close informed his colleagues that he could beat 'em both on the same night. And he was convinced, utterly convinced, that he could.

Not that Brian Close idly boasted of his abilities. His strength was tremendous, and it was more than matched by his courage. His leadership might have been erratic but it never lacked guts and drive. He might swear at his team, pursue some extraordinary tactic to its bitter end, yet he never lost his popularity as a man. You could tolerate a great deal from someone who fought so hard to win. His ordeal against Michael Holding at Old Trafford in 1976 demonstrated his resilience, his tenacious refusal at 45 years of age to back down one inch. It was as if his very manhood was being challenged. He allowed a succession of devastating deliveries to pound into his chest. He survived, bruised but not unbowed. I watched this terrifying episode on the BBC highlights that night. Graham Burgess and Mervyn Kitchen were in the room, too. We were diving under the sheets as if it were a Hitchcock movie. And we were 100 miles away!

Less well known is the postscript to the Old Trafford Test. Close played for Somerset in a Gillette Cup game next day. His chest was badly bruised. He was struck on it by Willis and buckled at the knees. Instantly he stood up again to continue his innings. It scarcely needs saying that he emerged as Somerset's top scorer that day.

But courage can be a dangerous friend. Close utterly refused to back down or to admit fault, whatever the weight of opinion might be. His attempts to sweep Benaud in 1961 were callously condemned by E. W. Swanton, yet regarded as worthwhile risks by Benaud. His loss of the England captaincy for his delaying tactics at Edgbaston followed his downright refusal to admit either that Yorkshire had prevaricated (to put it mildly!) or that prevarication was unfair. Ironically, and Brian Close's cricketing life was full of irony, Close had the previous winter suggested the implementation of a '20 overs in the final hour' rule. It was introduced one year too late to save his job. Somerset players well remember Close's lament, after rain had reduced Somerset's 1977 Gillette Cup semi-final against Middlesex to a 15-over farce and as he realised that his last chance of success had withered and died, that 'my life has been a series of cock-ups'.

Brian Close was not usually a self-analytical man. He did not grasp the humour of the things that happened to him. Stories about Close rely upon the image of the Old Blighter chewing gum, standing hands on knees at short leg, growling. His comment to Tom Cartwright, made as Gary Sobers walked out to bat, was not intrinsically hilarious. Yet everyone laughed uproariously at the time. Close strode knowingly to Cartwright, full of earthy wisdom and wily experience, and said as if it were a brilliant insight, 'Now, Tom, this lad's a left-hander!'

And at Torquay during a Sunday League game, Close informed his partner of his intention to swipe at every ball bowled by Surrey's Michael Hooper to the invitingly short mid-wicket boundary. Two sixes were hit, so Hooper dropped one a shade shorter. Close swept massively, edging the ball into his mouth. Teeth and blood scattered everywhere. Close repaired to the dressing room, sipping whisky to dampen pain. Next day he returned to Taunton to continue the Championship match. He sat miserably in his corner, grimacing with each shaft of pain, unable to eat or speak. Maurice Hill, who knew nothing of the injury, entered the room clutching his jaw and whispering 'Hell-fire, I've got toothache this morning!' Bette Davis never matched Close's anguished glare at Hill.

A postscript to this story, too. Close scored a century that day.

These things happened to Brian Close. He had a reckless quality that attracted incident as the candle attracts the moth. Only Close could walk through a glass door (he did not notice it!) and escape unhurt as he did at Westcliff. Only Close could decide to keep wicket with bare hands in a vital Gillette Cup game (apparently the injured Jim Parks' gloves did not fit!).

Yet his 'damn the consequences' determination was not selfish. Close was not a mean-spirited man, he neither cheated nor passed harsh judgements. Well, not often at any rate. If an umpire handed down an unfavourable verdict a storm might follow. One umpire who did was described, a few minutes later, as 'a nice man, but he'll have to go, you know'. He's still with us!

It is said that Close only ever complained about pain once. In a hospital it was. He was having his shoulder put back in joint. He grumbled to the nurse that he was in agony, and the nurse rebuked him, saying, 'There's a mother upstairs having twins and she's not making a fuss.' To which Close retorted, 'Well put them back in and see how she likes it!'

Despite these stories, Brian Close was not a figure of fun, far from it. He was not a humorous man in the least. He brought a hard core of competitive fight to Somerset. On the field he roared, cajoled, dived and jumped in his efforts to inspire victory. Yet off it, he was very much a loner. He stayed in a hotel room in Taunton, leaving his family in the North for the summer. He usually ate alone. Nor did he say much in the dressing room, living in a self-contained world of cricket and horses. Mostly he studied the *Sporting Life*, urging on various horses tipped by a mysterious figure known to us as 'Jackie Lad'. These animals invariably seemed to come second, often through incredible bad luck. As a result of this remoteness his team kept a respectful distance. Apart from the repeated request to 'fetch us a cup of tea, lad', Close remained, not aloof, but a little removed. His stature, physical and mental, ensured that no liberties were taken.

Certainly you concentrated very, very hard if you were batting with him or fielding to his bowling. It was not wise to run him out. On his return to Yorkshire he received an emotional standing ovation from 10,000 admirers. It was somehow inevitable that he should soon be cursing and dusting off dirty whites, as he strode furiously back to the pavilion having been run out. And at Oxford poor Steve Wilkinson called, 'Yes, no, wait, sorry', leaving Close sprawling on the turf having just scrambled to safety. He did not bother to rise, he turned a balding head and berated Aggro for a considerable time, a sight well worth seeing.

With that uncompromising determination to win it is not so surprising that Brian Close's life was full of drama. He was not one to rationalise, but relied upon decisions made upon the instant and defended them later come what may. His actions were never malicious, his anger was hot-blooded and healthy. Those on-the-field rows with Ian Botham (see Chapter 2) fairly shook the ground from time to time, orchestrated by much gesticulating, yet both men retain an abiding affection for the other. Possibly they are two of a kind: strong, aggressive, irrational but loyal, honest and popular. Certainly neither Ian nor Brian Close is exactly convinced by criticism. Close's skin grew thicker, but it's hard to imagine him threatening to thump some idiot of the Press.

Nor did failure weaken Close, as it does not cause Ian to blush like a maiden. The Old Blighter could produce endless explanations for dismissal, ranging from forgetting his chewing gum or wearing the wrong boots to stupid partners or foolish spectators jumping up and down as the bowler bowled. His most remarkable excuse came at Nottingham. After seven fruitless hours toiling in the field at Trent Bridge, Somerset batted. Brian Stead took wickets with successive balls in the first over. Richard Cooper, returning to the pavilion after his brief knock, exchanged words with Close. Nottingham set an attacking field for the hat-trick ball as Close took guard. Amazingly, Close swung lustily at his first ball, skying it straight to the solitary outfielder, Nirmal Nannan. Amidst astounded celebrations Close strode from the field, stormed into the changing room and roared at Cooper, 'Tha told me it were swingin', but tha never said it were seamin' too!' Brian Close could outstare any mere facts.

One other thing Botham and Close have in common. Both drive like South Americans (Fittipaldi, say). Those of us who have seen the hedge upon which Close once deposited his car are still confused as to how he could possibly have strayed so far from the road. Word has it that he was twiddling the radio searching for a race with one hand, fiddling with the *Sporting Life* with another and driving with the rest! Apparently the approaching bend escaped his notice. And, it is said, he did not abandon the wrecked vehicle until the race was over and his horse beaten.

I only travelled with the Godfather once. We spent most of the journey whizzing up the inside lane of the motorway, flashing past all those slow-coaches who were clogging up the fast lane! I followed him once, too. Colin Dredge and I, searching anxiously for a route to Chelmsford, chanced upon Close's car. We tagged courageously onto his tail. He did not notice us but we followed anyhow. It was when we ended up at the Brighton exit of the South Circular with Close waving his arms around at all and sundry that we realised something was amiss. We did not rely upon Close's concentration or sense of direction again.

But, for all his foibles, a deep warmth for Close survives in cricket. He could not be matched for courage or inspiration. His unconscious humour and tough approach survives, too. In my first Championship game I scored 46. After my dismissal our chairman, Len Creed, approached Close and observed, 'Young Roebuck played well, didn't he, Brian?' To which our intrepid hero replied, 'Ah, Len lad, there you are. What have you got for the 3.30 at Plumpton?'

But he had been watching, you know. He told me, 'Well played, lad, but tha should have scored a century.'

16

In Barbados

It's a very small island. Joel Garner drove me around it in an after-noon, stopping to show me some of the sights. He guided me through the Botanical Gardens, naming each plant, herb or tree we passed. On the streets every group waved to Joel, and he could name most of them, too. As Joel flew by, men lounging in the shade of a small bar alongside the road would call 'Joel Garner?', 'Big Bird?'. He'd growl 'Right', 'Hey', 'Easy, man' or 'Cool'. Or maybe he'd simply smile and toot as he drove on.

Children, dressed in immaculate uniforms belying a poverty be-trayed only by an absence of shoes, would smile shyly as we wriggled through them. One daring lad shouted 'You're slow, Garner!' amidst giggles, before hastily retreating into a mass of faces. As our tour continued, Joel offered lifts to ladies carrying baskets, and once in a while a large West Indian mama would pile into the car, delighted to find relief from the usual four-mile hike to the grocer's.

Joel is famous in Barbados; everyone recognises the cricketers on this intimate island. It is a proud island, too, proud of its stature in cricket. Butcher, Sobers, Nurse, Hall, Hunte, Garner: an extra-ordinary array of talent for so small a population. Visitors sometimes suspect that this pride borders on arrogance, a disdain of non-Bajan cricketers. Certainly Gloucestershire, with whom I was touring, were not taken too seriously and the games attracted little attention. Mind you, everyone knew the scores. If I mentioned my name anywhere, they'd respond, 'Oh, man, de fellow scoring de runs' (or not, as the case might be!).

Cricket is followed with intense interest, and no-one seems interested in much else. On my return to England I had to ring Vic Marks to catch up on world news, which had not featured prominently in my Bajan paper. 'Tell me, Vic lad,' I said, 'has a war broken out?' 'Yes,' he replied! It took me some time to realise he was deadly serious; I knew nothing of Iraq's invasion of Iran.

Cricket is desperately important in the West Indies. Viv Richards knows that news of his scores will filter back to Antigua, he knows he must be on his mettle. In their one-man knock-out, Viv was very keen to beat Barry Richards. It was unthinkable for him to lose to the champion of South Africa – what would they say back home? Luckily Barry did not give a damn who won, so Viv's conscience was appeased.

West Indies cricketers do have contact with a wide range of fellow countrymen. Viv Richards, with whom everyone, young and old, had been to school (and most had done his prep!), receives everyone from dustman to Prime Minister in his house in St John's. All are welcomed. Barbados has more heroes, but cricketers still do not lose touch with their roots. Until very recently, Joel Garner lived in a small house with his grandmother, a mile beyond Christ Church. Desmond Haynes lived with his mother in a ramshackle rum shop on a dirty street. We drank there one evening.

Bajan cricketers do have status, though, being one of the few groups able to break the chains of subsistence living. They may drive elegant cars and live in stone houses. Joel has designed and helped build a magnificent villa overlooking the west coast, and drives along in regal dignity. Mind you, he could live on a mountain and he would still contrive to be the social centre of life. On our return from our journey Big Bird asked his grandmother who had called. 'Oh, so many, Joel, so many,' she sighed. 'I can't remember any of their names.' No doubt they'd discover him in a night club later in the evening.

Barbados has produced a succession of fast bowlers. The Island team could include Garner, Marshall, Clarke, Alleyne, Daniel, Holder and Moseley. Few spinners have developed, though. They are not taken altogether seriously – mere pop-guns to be used when the heavy artillery is resting. Playing on the club grounds in Barbados, it is easy to see why Bajan cricket has become dominated by fast bowlers and big-hitting batsmen. Short boundaries and long grass prevail. If you hit the ball along the carpet it does not go far as the grass is thick and long. To score runs batsmen must wallop mighty sixes or sneak singles. With temperatures often soaring into the 90s and beyond it is not a difficult choice. I tried the singles. I scored 72 in 30 overs in the island of Barbados, amongst the cane-fields where the brunt of the heat is not tempered by sea breezes. I almost expired. In those conditions I'd either learn to hit the ball high and hard or take up darts. Conditions do determine technique, especially conditions encountered in formative years. Vic Marks, an off-side carver, built his game in a garden in which a greenhouse dominated the leg-side. I, an on-side nibbler, first batted in a back yard with a shed fielding in the covers. One learnt to adapt early in life, to avoid broken windows or damaged daffodils.

Even the Kennington Oval, the pride of Barbados, is an extraordinary ground to English eyes. I saw it before it was dressed for a Test match, saw it as a School Inspector might see a school were he to arrive a week early. It was shabby, dirty and apparently derelict. The dressing room was appalling, worse even than Somerset's at Weston-super-Mare. Most surprising, the square consisted of three strips to be used for Test matches, Shell Shield games, club games and nets for all of these. Apparently the grass grows almost overnight, so hot is the sun, so damp is the climate. Artificial surfaces are unheard of in these parts. The West Indian who was asked whether he preferred astro-turf or grass replied, 'Don't know, man. I've never smoked astro-turf!'

But if the grounds are small, surrounded by trees, the crowds are large and vocal. They sit in the shade of the branches, idling under the palm or the ash. A cacophony of chatter and laughter accompanies every ball, and comments fly out to the batsmen. Sometimes players join in the fun. Gregory Armstrong (lately of Glamorgan), who evidently turned out for every club in Barbados, would announce his intentions to all and sundry as he awaited his knock. He would lash the ball everywhere. Invariably his innings were spectacular. Alas, they were usually brief, too. He'd return to the pavilion utterly unabashed, astounded by his failure, laughing with his audience at his ineptitude.

Advice to the umpires is offered as well. Only brave men don the white coat in Barbados. It is a hazardous undertaking. One fellow, caught behind after an appalling swing, stood still, shaking in fury as the umpire raised an admonitory finger. He hurled his bat and gloves in the air, exclaimed 'No way, man' and 'You're crazy' and headed off at a snail's pace. He was greeted with a wise mixture of tactful sympathy and uproarious jollity.

Cricket is certainly different in Barbados: it is an exciting, explosive game. My mate, Bill Snowdon, a dour Lancastrian, opens the innings for Wanderers, a leading club. Bill is a bit of a blocker, to be frank. A couple of intransigent forward prods brings a hail of 'Beat de ball, man', 'Hook it, man, hook it', 'You asleep, Snowdon?' and, finally, an exasperated 'You dead, Snowdon?' Solid Snowdon starts are not yet an accepted part of Barbados cricket. As a raucous, disrespectful spectator shouted, 'Hey, Snowdon, you got two shots, de block and de big block'. Bill turned to me and muttered, 'They're idiots here, you know, idiots.' It was the cry of the defiant English professional whose pride has been dented by raw talent and rude comment.

17

On A Rainy Day

At first everyone is joyful. Dennis Breakwell is usually first on the scene. Awakened by spatters of rain, he rushes to the ground as dawn breaks, with a haunted look in his eyes like a Kamikaze pilot on his fifth mission. We all arrive earlier when the weather is wet, to debate the prospects for the day. If we are due to bat, several of our batsmen prod and poke the pitch, shaking their heads sadly, fixing visors as Corporal Jones fixes his bayonet. After rain at Hove, and fearing the prospect of batting on a treacherous 'sticky', one of our players doctored the scorebook with the probable result:

	SOMERSET	
	(first innings)	
B. C. Rose	retired hurt	0
S. M. Gavaskar	returned to Bombay	0
P. M. Roebuck	absent (in Gert's)	0
P. W. Denning	lost (searching for autographed bats)	0
I. T. Botham	not out	0
V. J. Marks	knocked out	0
D. Breakwell	heart attack on way to wicket	0
D. J. S. Taylor	'Tommy' sneezed, wife sent for him	0
K. F. Jennings	severe hangover	0
C. H. Dredge	Mandy said Colin couldn't bat	0
H. R. Moseley	lost spectacles, couldn't find bat	0

Not that it rains much at Taunton. Heart-rending tales of storms in Weston, hail in Wells and floods in Frome provoke anger at the pathetic efforts of the clouds around the County Ground. The number of times encouragingly black clouds gather over the High Street, only to meander feebly down the Tone, causes much distress in the Somerset camp. Fishing hooks are cast out of windows to drag escaping clouds back over the cricket pitch. Prayers are offered to the Almighty above us (and I don't mean Joel), or Gavaskar is sent out to do a rain dance. It is with much timidity, especially since the Bishop of Bath and Wells is a noted Somerset supporter, that I must report that Gavaskar has proved by far the more successful petitioner. At one stage the Apaches made a substantial offer for his services. This followed his superb effort in producing rain after the West Indies had batted and before any of us had the chance to face Marshall, Roberts and Croft. Inevitably, Gavaskar went too far in the end. In trouble at Bath, we begged Sunil to save us with rain. It poured down minutes later. Alas, once he had opened the taps he failed to close them, and it rained for four days! After that he was sacked for over-zealous performance of his duties.

Most cricketers affect an enthusiasm for rain. I daresay accountants enjoy it when their abacus breaks down, preventing work. In some cases the affection is genuine. As an amateur I played with Peter Robinson and Steve Wilkinson for Somerset 2nd XI. Peter used to peer out of the dressing room, issuing a running commentary on the approach of 'scouts' (clouds sent ahead of storms to warn of rain). Steve always preferred racing anyhow, disliking cricket as a distraction from the *Sporting Life*. With both men, rain provided relief from worry, a delay for possible failure and the ruin of career that it brings.

Anyhow it's wet today, even at Taunton. Reports indicate that we'd not play for a week in Glastonbury. Can't we transfer our headquarters there? Still, puddles are spreading on the square and the outfield is squelchy. It dries appallingly quickly at Taunton. In 1979 it rained all night during the Indian game but we started on time next day. But my, that rain is teeming down. No play today, surely? No chance of any of us venturing onto the field to mop up the wet patches, as Cowdrey did in the 1968 Ashes series. Several of our players need to be restrained from going out with hoses and watering cans!

The umpires knock and enter to inform the assembled crew that it is wet and play will be delayed. This provokes rather more cheers than tears. King Lear has long been a particular hero of ours with his

On A Rainy Day

'Blow, winds, and crack your cheeks. Rage, blow!
You cataracts and hurricanoes, spout
Till you have drenched our steeples, drowned the cocks.'

Not abandoned though, just delayed. If a Sahara sun appears we might start at 4.30 pm. It's only 10.30 am now. Cheerfulness vanishes. Umpires are sworn at, cajoled and begged. Can't we go home? No chance – we must hang on until there is not a hint of a possibility of play. We know that, but it does the heart good to grumble.

So we settle into our dressing room. At least it is brighter than our old one, hidden in a Victorian pavilion. Our previous pavilion still stands proud and erect if rather well-worn, like Dick Emery's Old Etonian fallen on hard times. It is protected by orders from all sorts of people who've never been inside it. When a shed near it caught fire it is rumoured that a Somerset committee man rushed around suggesting that petrol not extinguishers be poured upon the blaze. He was joking, but it's a thought.

We'll have to entertain ourselves for a few hours. Doing what? Some opt for cards: brave men, these. All games between Somerset professionals sooner or later degenerate into rugby. Our pre-season soccer, basketball, volleyball and touch rugby inevitably end in heated disputes. Cards is no soft option, it's like playing Russian Roulette with Hell's Angels. Marks, Jennings, Rose and Denning start a game. Rose plays with an air of ethereal wisdom, Marks with earthy common sense. Comments fly around: 'By your face you've either got a great hand or the biggest load of rubbish ever'; 'What sort of a lead is that?'; and the misleading 'See one, play one' as a six is followed up with a jack. Jennings and Denning start cheating, to add sparkle to the game. Things warm up. 'Crap' is replaced by 'cheat', a far more suitable game.

No, cards are to be avoided. Botham might join in, and someone will end up whitewashed, or in the bath, or both. Of course if Botham is not playing cards he must be doing something else somewhere else. Possibly he's thumping someone, or putting ice-cubes in socks. Botham in a dressing room on a wet day resembles a caged lion, roaring and pacing around, searching for life.

Jerry Lloyds switches on his radio, adding tinny pop music to the bedlam. As a Monkees record is played he observes, 'They're still very big in Australia.' Keith Jennings asks, 'What are they, gorillas?' That's about the level of communal humour. It wears a bit thin after a while, as Dennis Breakwell repeats and repeats various ditties which I could not possibly reproduce here. Colin Dredge, who rarely utters a word, wanders to the refreshment room to request 'a crocodile sandwich, and make it snappy'! Otherwise few laughs today.

Apart from the worry as to where Botham will next spring, things settle down. Joel is sprawled across the settee, contriving to occupy every seat with an arm or a leg. He dozes fitfully, or reads a thriller. Hallam Moseley and Viv Richards are in the back room, sleeping. Derek Taylor chats away to the opposition. He is a compulsive chatterer who revels in recalling past heroes. He enjoys gossiping to cricketers of his era. Alas, this excludes the rest of Somerset – Grace and Spofforth mean little to us – so he pops into the away team's room for a really satisfying natter!

Cups of coffee and pork pies are passed around. 'Was there any racing in Taunton last week?' wonders Breakwell, grimacing at his pie. Rain hammers down on the roof, thankfully not made of tin which used to get everyone far too excited. Puddles are nearly lakes now. Too wet for golf? Probably not; these self-same men would play golf in a blizzard. Some are very good at that strange game. Rose is an elegant striker of the ball, Botham has a prodigious slice and a surprisingly delicate touch, Taylor is short but straight (in his golf, I mean), Slocombe and Lloyds at least resemble noble golfers to the uninitiated eye. Most of the rest of us are willing hackers, Denning, Roebuck, Marks and Richards (who disguises a hacker's returns with a champion's demeanour). We did play in Dublin once. I went round with Marks and Popplewell. Pops and I were first intrigued, then startled, by the measured intensity with which Marks prepared for each of his many shots. He'd stand staring, no, glaring, at the ball, head tucked deep into his arms. He held this position for fully 10 seconds as his partners desperately resisted a tide of laughter. Alas, the dam broke on the second tee, and poor Vic was never the same again as stifled hilarity greeted each stroke.

Still everything is quiet – as the cowboys say, 'too damn' quiet'. It can't last.

It doesn't. Botham lurches in, with a demonic glint in his eye. Soon grubby socks fly through the air, with Gard and Denning in their wake. West Indians are awoken, grumpily muttering. Efforts to deflect him to the visitors' room fail. A wild atmosphere prevails, disrupting the stupor into which we were gradually sinking. Cards are upset, tomatoes are ducked, bodies hide behind couches. Anything could happen.

It does. But eventually the dust settles. As in the aftermath of other great battles, an uneasy peace prevails. The silence is uncanny. We sit around choosing various teams. We select an Ugly XI, a Nasty XI, a Nice Chaps XI, a Round the Twist XI, a Rotund XI. Selections include cricketers from all counties. An ex-Somerset captain finds his way, amidst much hilarity, into every team. And he's captain of most of them!

Lunch is taken early. Taunton is a quagmire. Our groundsman, in a tremendous gesture of solidarity, says we'll not play until July. Our obdurate umpires at last abandon play for the day. We head home, praying secretly for sunshine 'tomorrow and tomorrow and tomorrow'.

18

Arthur Milton

Arthur played most of his two decades of county cricket in those halcyon days before the Sunday League, before each team had someone very big, very black and very fast. Those must have been well-mannered days, with less wild appealing, with 'walking' widely observed, with half-volleys bowled to tail-enders, and with helmets but a twinkle in Mike Brearley's eye.

Arthur belonged to that era in which cricket was a battle of wits between craftsmen. If you did not learn your craft well enough, did not study and sweat, you would not long survive. True, crowds were poor, cricket was dying on its feet. But crowds, sponsors, men of commerce, were not thought to be necessary. Cricket was for cricketers, a duel of skills, an exposition of craftsmanship. Blacksmiths and watchmakers do not require audiences, and nor did off-spin bowlers or opening batsmen.

Cricket was a simple game then. You played six days a week, six hours each day. Sundays were for roasts, for jaunts up the river, for games of golf. Saturday nights were for parties, they were not uneasy preludes to 40-over hits. That was Arthur's cricketing life. No briefcases, hardly even a tracksuit. Arthur was a rural English cricketer, travelling to the ground each day in his old banger. In some ways he was an English Doug Walters, for Walters hailed from the Australian bush. Walters is the hero of all Australian schoolboys, with his smoking, his cards, his modesty in success: an Aussie Clint Eastwood. Arthur (though scarcely resembling Clint Eastwood at all) is a mellow, very English hero, a mild Reginald Perrin, able to appreciate the absurdity of things, as much a part of the Cotswold Hills as the Empress is a part of Blandings Castle.

Arthur played his cricket with apparent ease, with a quiet confidence born of ability. He moved with deceptive speed, though always apparently at half-throttle – a most unnerving trait to more committed colleagues. Yet he was enough of an athlete, had enough touch, to play soccer for Arsenal and England (1951) and cricket for Gloucestershire and England (1958). Probably he will prove to be the last of the double internationals, unless Ian Botham's shooting improves and except, inevitably, for Vivian Richards who says he's played soccer for Antigua against Haiti. I gather Antigua barely got a kick!

You'd never guess Arthur was such a talented man if you met him. He has none of those star attributes. As a countryman at heart, he leads a relaxed, meek life. He utterly fails to dress like Elton John, to smoke cigars like Winston Churchill, to appear at first nights with Debbie Harry or to jig at discos with Susan George. A pint at the local is much more his colour of woad. Even in the Big City as an Arsenal player Arthur led a quiet life. He was a skilful, nippy winger in the Stanley Matthews mould. In his time with the Gunners he played with a youthful, balding D. B. Close who, needless to say, played as a barnstorming centre-forward to complement Arthur's subtle skills. To his manager's dismay, Close frittered away endless chances by heading the ball over the bar. He was sent to the practice ground to head endless crosses into the net. Next Saturday, Milton duly streaked past his full-back, slipped over a delicate cross to which Close rose majestically, bent back his thick neck and smacked the ball downwards. It bounced in front of the goal and soared over the bar just as before! I expect Close swore blind at this injustice, while Arthur chuckled wryly at the perversity of life.

Possibly Arthur lacked the ruthless, driving ambition to be quite the best at cricket or soccer. He appeared to jog along, strolling to success, deflecting a ball here or chipping it there. He was never remorselessly productive enough to protect his England position. When his chance came to open for England he scored a century. But he never consolidated, having the misfortune to tour Australia at the time of Meckiff. He reflects with a sigh that Meckiff merely ambled in to bowl, delivered a series of friendly half-volleys, then suddenly and with no apparent change of action bowled a ball of devastating pace. At any rate Arthur played the last of his six Test Matches in 1959. He never again supplied the weight of runs to demand a return to international cricket. His colleagues and opponents admired his superb technique on treacherous wickets but remarked that he did not always score heavily in favourable conditions.

Partly, no doubt, this failing was caused by Arthur's frustration at insipid cricket. He detested the dead wickets at Bristol with their lack of bounce. Batsmen could plod onto the front foot and acquire runs as bowlers struggled to generate life from the unhelpful pitch. Arthur could get pretty fed up with such poor-quality cricket and with the wickets that encouraged it, so he scored most of his runs away from Bristol, whilst lesser batsmen thrived in these reduced circumstances.

Not that Arthur could get very angry. At slip once, he picked up a low chance, holding it up to show the catch had been clean. 'I caught it, Peter,' he informed the batsman, Sainsbury of Hampshire. 'I'm not so sure about that,' replied the redoubtable Sainsbury. 'Oh well, stay in if you like,' said an exasperated Arthur. And he did. Not many cricketers would have reacted so mildly to having their good spirit doubted.

Arthur rarely made a fuss, he was too whimsical for that. David Green, Milton's opening partner for Gloucestershire, recalls Arthur introducing Mike Procter to greyhound racing. Gambling is one of Arthur's pastimes. He tips you a horse with the ethereal wisdom of a man who knows his stuff. You feel as if it is only modesty that prevents him from saying that the horse will win rather than 'Well it might, and it might not. It's got a chance, you know.' You back his tip, confident that the twinkling eye contains something approaching knowledge. Sometimes it does and sometimes it does not. If Arthur has heard mention that certain animals have developed an appetite for currant buns his tips might be of value. But usually the horse or dog is left at the start or is ridden by a blithering idiot or interfered with by a lamentably inferior greyhound.

Anyhow, David Green describes Arthur taking Procter along to his first dog meeting at Eastville. Apparently Arthur decided that a particular dog would win. He sent Procter to place £2 on no. 4 dog. Mike, a little over-excited by the new experience, and with a couple of black and tans on board, returned with a piece of paper betraying the fact that he'd put £4 on no. 2. Arthur received this intelligence with a few moments silence, and then launched into a tirade of the most colourful invective which was only stemmed when no. 2 dog romped home at 5 to 1. That is Arthur.

Upon his retirement, upset by Gloucestershire's failure to offer him a post he was far too reticent to request, he found himself coaching Oxford University. He brought a refreshingly mild approach to The Parks. If Vic Marks, not exactly a Genghis Khan himself, sought his advice as to the best course of action if the toss was won, Arthur would reply, 'Well, I'd either bat or bowl.' Yet he was a valued figure, pottering about, instilling confidence rather than analysing technique. He calmed edgy students, offering restrained advice rather than ultimate solutions.

He was not, perhaps, a zealous coach, preferring to leave well alone. But then he was not a zealous batsman either. As a rustic Cowdrey, he appeared uncannily relaxed at the crease. He treated the ball with immense, cheerful respect. Or he'd glide down the pitch without any obvious movement, resembling a nineteenth-century servant shuffling along in skirts. He guided the ball into gaps, rather as a golfer rolls in a putt. His strokes trickled along, somehow slipped between eager fieldsmen and bobbed along to the boundary. His bat never made that meaty sound celebrated by poets, it produced a sort of cloth noise as if the ball was wrapped in socks. Hence his nickname, 'Clothbat'. Not, you'll observe, Big Art or Prince Art, but Clothbat Arthur.

Arthur did bat in a flowing, discreet way. Violent, dramatic blows did not suit his temperament. David Green did once tease him into an unusually aggressive hit. Batting against Surrey, Green 'made a remark to the effect that someone as old and frail as he could not be expected to get more than two runs off any one blow. He fixed me for a moment with beady blue eyes, and walked back to face Pat Pocock, whose first delivery he charged like Ivanhoe and hoisted it high over wide long-on into the seats to the left of the pavilion.' I doubt if Arthur ever quite recovered from that hit. He makes as improbable an Ivanhoe as a one-legged Dudley Moore applying for the role of Tarzan.

Since his Oxford years Arthur has mellowed even more. He arises at 5 am each morning to deliver the post in his Cotswold village. He seems utterly content with such an independent, undramatic job. He lives with his family, only occasionally returning to Bristol for a pint with David Shepherd or David Allen. If you see him on his rounds, better not suggest the bags look a bit heavy for so old a man. He'll only fix you with that 'beady blue eye' and after that, anything might happen.

19

My First Night Game

I'd seen night cricket before of course, in the flesh at Sydney Cricket Ground. I'd sat on the hill with the Ockers in tee-shirts, shorts and thongs, sipping cans of Toohey's Lager, pretending to be an Aussie through and through, shouting 'have a go, yer mug', singing 'Come on, Aussie, come on' and chanting 'Brearley is a woman' with the guilt-ridden heart of St Peter as the cock crowed the third time.

A glorious splash of colour it had been, with the setting of the glowing red sun over the city's skyline, the climbing of the yellow moon into the black night above us, and a vibrant atmosphere – a spectacle to match the Edinburgh Tattoo. The crowd was happy and rollicking, depressed only by the Cripps-like limitation of each man to 24 cans of lager. Aussies scarcely loosen the throat for 24 lagers. Still the Hill was noisy, full of pungent comment and blunt wit. Each girl wandering by drew wolf-whistles from the night. One called out, 'Eric, where are you?' into the sea of bronze and tee-shirts, and cries of 'Here, love' spread happily around the Hill, adding to the confusion.

Oh yes, a happy time, night cricket. And warm, too, nice and warm. You hardly needed a shirt or trousers, not until late at any rate. Well, Somerset play their first night game today in Oxford. It's 28 April and we are at Oxford United soccer ground for a game of cricket against a side made up of players from local clubs. Playing cricket in the dark? And with white balls, black pads and blue gloves? There would be a few things to which to adapt but it could do no harm, could it? Might as well like it as lump it.

Arrival at the ground, bags, helmets and chewing gum in hand, brings our first surprise. For years we have imagined that soccer players live in an opulence beyond cricket. Night clubs, gambling, mistresses, gin – we are used to all these. But huge crowds, massive wages and tours to Majorca belong to the working man's game. To our astonishment the Oxford United dressing room proves to be dingy and decrepit, every bit as bad as our old rooms at Taunton. Mind you, we are in the away team's room. Perhaps the Oxford players are lying on sofas, sipping port and puffing on cigars. They might not win but they have more fun!

Our shirts hang on pegs around the room, just as we'd imagined. Only the absence of dubbin shows that there's new business afoot today. We are supposed to wear these soccer shirts so the crowd will be able to identify us. Not always a good idea, that! I don my no. 4 shirt, the shirt of Nobby Stiles and Franz Beckenbauer. Neither of them were Spurs players – and, alas, Blanchflower wore no. 6 if my memory serves me well. Will I clog and dart like Stiles or bestride the field with the cool elegance of Beckenbauer?

After changing, we potter out to inspect the pitch and to feel the atmosphere. The trip is enough to sow the first terrible seeds of doubt. It's damned cold, Scott of the Antarctic weather. We feel like Captain Oates as we shiver to the centre spot, where we have spied a strip of canvas and some stumps. We inspect the pitch and look at each other with glum foreboding. No particular effort has been made to flatten the surface. It is as crumpled as the sheets in Soho and it appears to be frozen, or at least part of it does. We bowl a few trial balls. One hits a crater and skids along the canvas. Another strikes a crevice and shoots up over our heads. Could be an interesting evening's batting! Our bowlers find the canvas so slippery that they are unable to run in to bowl. Obviously the footballers feel that if bumps and a wet surface are good enough for them, they're good enough for us. Tell that to David Bryant or Bjorn Borg.

Still, we must contrive to perform as well as possible without rupturing ourselves – the supporters have come to see good-quality cricket, not buffoons in white clowning around. It's not their fault that conditions are difficult. We return to the battle of the dressing room, immediately tear off soccer shirts and hunt for jumpers, vests, pyjamas – anything that will fit under the soccer jersey. We wear thermal underwear, long johns and tracksuits under our cricket trousers. Sydney Cricket Ground was never like this. It is April, of course, but soon the days will be too long to permit night cricket. It will always be a cold affair in England.

Nearly bowl-off time. *Match of the Day* music dances around the ground as spectators sip coffee and smoke cigarettes. They make quite a sizeable crowd, several thousand on a cold, dark, damp evening in Oxford, mostly dressed like Humphrey Bogart in *Casablanca*. How many will come when the novelty wears off? Our dressing room is a hive of activity. It must be the soccer shirts which raise the nervous tension. Somerset players are much more edgy before a soccer game than before, say, the Gillette Cup Final. Exercises are done, boots polished, hair combed, balls juggled, tactics discussed. Everyone just reads the paper or smokes a quiet fag before a cricket match.

Somerset CCC soccer players are a notoriously temperamental lot. One was known to pick up the ball if his team were losing and leave the field saying that it was his ball anyway. Another refused to carry on playing because 'No-one is passing to me, they just steam from one end to the other as if they were bulldozers.' Several fights have been recorded in pre-season soccer matches – yet no-one ever argues the toss over cricket!

Our captain risks the cold air to spin the coin. He wins. Should we bat now and freeze later or be done with the worst now and bat in the depths of the night? We decide to postpone the agony and tell our most junior players to strap on their black pads and blue gloves. Let the young 'uns hit up some runs whilst we gnarled, cantankerous old professionals warm up with a mug of Bournville or hot Marmite. We repair to the dug-out, our breath misting as it mingles with the cutting night air. Euphemistically speaking, the wicket is interesting but our volunteers are staunch. Jerry Lloyds and 'Palm' Olive do well, helped by the inability of the bowlers to stand up. They are a-slippin' and a-slidin' like Robin Cousins after 24 cans of lager.

We enjoy ourselves in the dug-out for the cricket is a bit nearer to Keystone Cops than we'd expected. It is good, clean, healthy fun, especially from the warmth of the dug-out. The Oxford United dug-out is not centrally heated (I doubt if even Liverpool's is built for comfort) but the cluster of cramped bodies generates heat for, as the Flanders and Swann song puts it, 'heat goes from the hotter to the cooler as a rula!' And the dug-out produces a bawl of football cries, shouts of 'Come on, ref', 'Penalty, penalty', 'Book him' and 'Send him off'. We send no. 3 out to do some exercises as the batting comes stodgy, just as Sir Alf might have done.

Our young 'uns do well, fuelled by the need to impress more secure colleagues. Seasoned professionals plan a rather more brief spell at the crease. Upon Lloyds' dismissal Joel strides to the wicket and essays a few gigantic swipes before rushing from the field with his stumps in disarray. To our sympathetic 'hard luck' he grins broadly and replies, 'That's good luck, man.' Ian Botham bats and fields in an assortment of scarves and Peter Denning finds a bobble-hat to warm his hair. Everyone searches for gloves to withstand frostbite.

Despite these varying tactics we score well. We hit lots of sixes to the cheers of the crowd. When I say that we hit lots of sixes, it is not a royal 'we'. I don't hit any sixes at all, probably wouldn't if we played in the back garden, either. But the rectangular shape of a soccer ground ensures that chips square of the wicket carry the field. Straight hits need more beef but not nearly enough to deter Ian Botham, who all but clears the floodlights with one vivid blow. Not that it's much use hitting the ball on the ground, as the long grass quickly drags it to a halt. I am cheered, though, by the prospect of scoring a five if I can hit a ball into the Oxford United goal.

Alas, all good things come hurriedly to an end. Our 25 overs finish with a clatter of wickets amidst the cheers of a keen and appreciative crowd. In the field, huddling beneath layers of feeble clothing, we rush enthusiastically through our overs. The ball seems mighty hard, and brittle fingers ignore firm strokes whenever dignity permits. Our bowlers skid in off a few paces, summoning sufficient venom to dismiss the club batsmen. Our young 'keeper has an awkward time of it as balls bundle along to him, ever ready to dive into a hole and dart up into his teeth. On soccer fields even the fieldsmen need helmets.

As the game fades I'm called upon to bowl. My first spell under lights, a proud moment. I curl down a cunning off-break whereupon the umpire calls 'Over' and I'm promptly thanked for my bowling. It appears that during my cold doze in the goal-mouth at long leg Peter Denning has been stolen to draw a raffle. (Does this happen at Lord's? Or on *Match of the Day?*) My role was merely to complete his over. If you have ever seen Peter Denning bowling you will realise just how subtle and profound an insult this was.

As the overs tick by, Nigel Popplewell, irrepressible as ever, contributes a few handstands. Most of us enjoy ourselves in a strange sort of way despite our usual grumblings. It's different, at any rate, and quite a sight. By 10 pm we have darted off the pitch into hot showers and are slowly recovering circulation. A hint of brandy, a sausage roll and back to the hotel in Oxford ready for the big game tomorrow.

It has all resembled one of those hot chocolate adverts. You remember them: a cold, cuddling couple running from a wet, wretched evening and huddling in front of log fire with slippers, poodle and a mug of hot chocolate, drinking chocolate. But was it wise for them to have gone out in the first place?

20

The Long, Black Telegraph Pole

A couple of nights before our 1979 Gillette Cup semi-final the Somerset players were entertained by one of our most devoted supporters, John Cleese. During the brief interludes when the players managed to escape the attentions of dead parrots, John Cleese was to be seen in deep and profound conversation with Joel Garner. This provoked a most diverting thought – could this be a new comedy team developing? Certainly both men have remarkable limbs, including several arms and legs each acting independently of all others. Perhaps they might start with a guest appearance on *Come Dancing*, offering a fresh approach to the Tango. Anyhow, let the Muppets beware.

John Cleese's comic abilities are well known and at least partly unconscious; Dennis Breakwell could scarcely control himself when Cleese attempted to pour him some wine. Perhaps the cork should have been removed first! That Joel Garner is a figure of similar hilarity is less well known. Indeed, most opposing batsmen seem quite unable to appreciate his talents: the somewhat improbable cohesion of Big Bird's arms and legs as he flaps in to bowl provokes not one whit of joy in these dour opponents. Not that they ignore him entirely. The more long-in-the-chewing-gum among them will greet Joel with a cheerful 'Good morning' and will add a sympathetic if trifle optimistic, 'A bit chilly for fast bowling, isn't it?' But apart from such pleasantries, few appreciate the range of Garner's talents.

Of course, there are good reasons for this widespread ignorance. For a start, it is almost impossible to understand anything Joel says. He talks in a strange lingo, presumably a broad Barbadian banter, which shares no words (so far as one can tell) with the mother tongue as she is spoken from Chewton Mendip to Nether Stowey. Consequently, conversation with Joel tends to be a hazardous business. Ask him for the time and his reply might vary from the earthy 'In the car park' to the wholly mystical 'Well, I haven't been there for a while'.

Naturally, being a fast bowler, Big Bird can afford to be a little elusive. He need only say a few words and follow with a great laugh for the whole dressing room to be in uproar. And when he pops into the visitors' room for a little social chit-chat, he enjoys a marvellously attentive audience. The room practically falls apart at the slightest hint of a witticism. Fast bowlers are treated with the most touching affection.

Big Bird rather likes being so very black, so very large and so very difficult to decipher. He feels no obligation to hide his considerable light under a nearby bushel (not that they make bushels like that nowadays) like some reluctant debutante (and where have they all gone?). He fairly relishes using his long reach to best advantage in a darts game, placing rather than propelling his darts into the board. After a particularly successful day he will stroll around the main streets of Taunton with the whites of his eyes and gleaming teeth visible for miles around, thoroughly pleased with the glances of astonished children and terrified babies. Or, if there's a bit of a crowd in, Joel will charge around the boundary with kangaroo strides, pick up the ball in one gigantic hand and hurl it as far as possible in the general direction of the stumps. If, perchance, wicket-keeper Derek Taylor is the correct distance away, the ball will land with a thud in his gloves. If not, well at least the crowd will appreciate the spectacle of the throw and the sight of fielders diving around, some trying to stop the ball, others desperate to avoid its perilous path.

This slightly mischievous use of his powers sometimes extends to Joel's batting. As with most fast bowlers, Big Bird is immensely impressed by his own style. Often he talks of his desire to 'flick' the ball here and to 'lick' it there. Occasionally the most ambitious strokes succeed gloriously, for instance when Les Taylor was despatched for a powerful straight six at Leicester as Joel tried to coax victory from defeat. Even if success eludes him, Joel is well worth watching at the crease, particularly when in tandem with Derek Taylor. Derek runs in very short, scampered steps which contrast dramatically with Big

Bird's massive strides and frequently leave him in danger of being lapped.

Actually Joel's batting has developed these past two years. No longer do we ponder upon his ability to lift the ball very high but not very far. The nine iron has been abandoned for the wood, and Joel lashes the ball very hard and very straight these days. Some of his strokes 'on the up' at Bath in 1981 were worthy of the master himself, and neither the master nor the rest of us any longer doubt Big Bird when he announces his intention to smite 50 in 10 overs.

Not that Joel is an exuberant West Indian fast bowler every day. Cheerful times are interspersed with periods of reflective silence during which Joel retires behind one of the thrillers he reads so voraciously (or *The Gulag Archipelago* if the mood is really black). If these dark thoughts do surface it is usually to express frustration at authorities who govern without sensitivity. Joel has an astute, lively mind and can be angered by thoughtless administrators who make demands that he feels to be unfair. Big Bird is a thorough professional who does his job as well as he is able, which is very well, and he does not appreciate interference from amateurs. It is, perhaps, just as well that he is discreet, for Joel is not one to bed down early at the beckoning of selectors or chairmen. Before Somerset's 1979 Gillette Cup victory Joel was in a night club, quietly drinking and chatting until the early hours of the morning. He knew he would not sleep if he obeyed the curfew, but realised he would perform much better if he slept for six hours rather than tossing and turning for nine.

Joel does have an independent, self-reliant nature. He designed and built his own villa in Barbados and then brought off a remarkable coup by immediately renting it at a high fee to American bankers. Big Bird's anger at authorities is surprising in many ways. He has repeatedly shown himself to have a cool, detached temperament. He responds with neither words nor gestures to the most provocative attack by opponent or spectator. Should a fast bowler be so sadly misled as to whistle a bouncer past Joel's ears (no mean feat in itself), Big Bird will merely smile benevolently down the pitch as if to say (as might the frog to the tadpole), 'Your turn will come.' Another Somerset bowler has been known, in similar circumstances, to inform the ill-advised bowler, 'if you had another brain cell, you'd be a plant' – but that's not Joel's style.

Nor does Joel permit himself the luxury of being upset by crowds. At Harrogate a supporter addressed some unpleasant remarks to Big Bird as he lolloped out to bat (just when, as chance would have it, the groundsman was warming up the heavy roller). Rather than give any indication that he had so much as heard these remarks, let alone been hurt or angered by them, Joel proceeded to bat with aplomb, contributing a flamboyant 53 before bowling some distinctly hasty overs to Boycott and Lumb.

So despite his keen intelligence, Joel is far too full of fun to be irritated for long. He prefers to quieten raucous spectators by performance rather than repartee. He bears no malice, though he lies in wait for a couple of people who did him wrongs years ago. Lancashire rejected him in 1978 and one of their players reported, 'Garner can't bowl.' That man has not scored too many runs against Somerset since!

In fact Joel is so cool, so dispassionate, that his colleagues try to steam him up by passing on supposedly overheard comments. Viv Richards once whispered to Joel that he'd heard Alan Ealham say, 'Garner isn't fast, though he does obtain steep bounce.' Read Chapter 25 on the Somerset v. Kent game in 1979 to see the damaging results! We'll never know if Ealham ever said anything of the sort, of course.

It is easy to underestimate Joel. His talents are wide-ranging. As he lives two houses down from me, I've learned to appreciate his cooking, his delicate typing, the scope of his reading, his hospitality (as Clyde Walcott said, 'Richards is king of the cricket, but Garner is king of the night!') and his mowing (quite a sight!).

It is just as easy, and far more deadly, to under-rate his bowling. His run-up is short and his delivery deceptively effortless. But no colleague or opponent of Joel will deny that he is one of the very fastest bowlers in the world. Certainly he is one of the most awkward, hammering the ball into the grass from a height far above sight-screens which were built with less prodigious mortals in mind. Joel generates remarkable bounce from apparently docile pitches and has the ability to change pace without any noticeable change of action. With these abilities it is not easy to decide whether Joel most resembles Jeff Thomson or Tom Cartwright. Like Thomson, he is capable of bouncing the ball from a good length into the batsman's ribs and of maintaining a menacing hostility on slow pitches. And, like

Cartwright, he can produce controlled movement in either direction (not at the same time, unless bemused victims are to be believed, but often in the same delivery) without sacrificing line and length.

Perhaps the truth is that Big Bird will bowl like Cartwright when the mood so takes him and like Thomson if he feels sharp and aggressive. In the West Indies team, Joel is usually used as a stock bowler to hold the fort while Roberts, Holding, Daniel, Marshall et al are resting: it may be that this use of Joel is founded on a shrewd appreciation of his nature, with his relatively mild temperament and whole-hearted dislike of conceding runs.

As a defensive bowler Joel is well-nigh supreme. Few others could bowl at the end of a thriving Sunday League innings to Allan Lamb and Peter Willey with seven men in behind the bat. Nor are many bowlers of his pace as willing to bowl long spells for their team – not many fast bowlers would have volunteered to bowl all afternoon and evening one hot Harrogate day to save their side from defeat. It is never difficult to persuade Big B to bowl but sometimes it can be hard to stop him.

No doubt Joel will play cricket for only a few years more. He enjoys himself in Taunton but longs for a leisurely life on the beaches of Barbados with the friends from his days of poverty. He vows never to return to the huts and rags of his youth, and with his shrewd business sense he never will. But until he retires, the 'long, black telegraph pole' will continue to grace the cricket fields of the world with his disciplined bowling, his flamboyant strokeplay and his wide, cheerful smile.

21

And On The Seventh Day . . .

Sunday. The Sabbath. It's supposed to be a day of rest. Not for me. We're playing Middlesex in the John Player League today.

Struggle out of bed. Open curtains. Not a cloud in the sky. Not even a few scouts. We'll play all right.

Potter downstairs to pinch the Sunday papers. Think of 'phoning Keith Jennings. He feels ill every Sunday morning. He says it's nerves. Strange. He feels OK when he leaves the Globe. And, if he finds his key, his house and his bed, sleeps pretty well, too.

This is the way to live. Sunday papers all morning, reading every word. Study article on Somerset Maugham in *The Observer*, but keep peeping at *Sunday People* story about nude vicars rampaging around Brighton on motor-cycles chased by policemen in drag on horses. Wonder if Sussex need any new players.

Back to the papers after coffee. Preparing for a juicy roast lunch with wine and Yorkshire pudding. Then port, slippers and a doze in front of *The Big Match*.

Alas, not today. At noon it's time to drive to Taunton. Must arrive early to avoid the frenzied crush of Sunday at the County Ground.

Listen to Beethoven's Pastoral on the journey – anything to prolong the illusion of tranquillity.

Arrive. Abandon all hope that no-one will venture forth to enjoy my efforts to survive the pandemonium of 40-over cricket. I expect the Christians cherished similar despairing hopes before their meetings with the lions. Diving. Running. Jumping. Chasing. Throwing.

Can't Middlesex invade Libya or somewhere so that I can boycott the game?

Fielding on Sundays is a recurrent nightmare. I dream I'm fielding at Old Trafford. I collect an edge at fine leg. I mean to return it to Derek Taylor. At the last second I choose the bowler as my target. I assume I've adjusted my sights. Then, as I throw the ball, I consider the 'keeper's end to be preferable after all. I adjust my aim 22 yards to Derek Taylor's right, towards third man, miles from anyone. The ball careers off to the boundary with a startled Viv Richards in hot pursuit. The crowd roars its approval and the Lancashire team look pleased as well.

Then I wake up trembling and remember it's all true. The story has become something of a legend at Somerset. Even now as I shape to field a ball on Sundays, colleagues at all parts of the ground act as if placed on red alert. By the way I'm studied by new Lancashire players as if I were the ninth wonder of the world, I gather the tale has not altogether died in Manchester either.

Salad for lunch. Really, I must turn Catholic. An Englishman has roast for lunch on Sunday. Everyone knows that.

I buy a scorecard. Perhaps they'll leave me out today. A confused feeling. I'd be very disappointed not to play, yet cling to the possibility as the greenfly cling to my roses.

If I were left out, I'd go for a stroll around town. Far too tense to watch. I'd end up swearing at umpires, opponents, friends, spectators and the heavens above us. Much easier playing, and much more fun.

Bit of a knock-up with 'Vic lad'. The 'lad' is inherited from Brian Close, who called everyone 'lad' – hence 'Pete lad', 'Ian lad' and, on one famous occasion, 'Ethel lad' (possibly a reference to Ethel lad the Unready. And who can blame him?).

I ask Vic Marks what line he's going to bowl. He asks me where I'm going to slog Daniel. We both laugh.

'Rosey' comes towards me. He looks worried and forlorn. My heart leaps, obviously he is dreading breaking the news to me that I'm not playing. Remind myself to look a broken man. 'You're playing, Rupert,' he says. 'Right, skipper,' I reply in true Biggles fashion. Very pleased. Caterpillars begin to munch away in my stomach. You don't deserve butterflies if you have salad for lunch on Sundays.

Cigarettes, received from John Player, are distributed. Gillette provide razors for the players (shave if you win, cut throat if you lose).

By now the ground is full and 'Rosey's army' is in full cry. Everyone practises his fielding. I study their players. They're all international class. And the bowlers! Van der Bijl, Edmonds, Emburey, Selvey and Daniel. Hell, where *am* I going to hit Daniel?

22

A Day As A Fast Bowler

I'd always wanted to be a fast bowler, the terror of the team, just as a punch-bag must fancy being a pugilist. To stride around, shirt clinging to hairy chest, with an 'and you can get stuffed, too' glint in the eye. To arrive at the annual Cricketers' Association meeting and provoke astonished glances, to affect the sort of entry that sends Dennis Breakwell scurrying back to Taunton to report that 'some more big blokes have been signed, and they all had mean eyes and bulging biceps'. To cause Dennis's moustache to twitch even half as much as it did when he first saw Vincent Van der Bijl in the flesh. Who could ask for more?

To receive kid-glove treatment as the skipper, a tyrant with lesser mortals, begs you to put in a burst of fire. To enter the visitors' room and be received with cheery warmth, as Mervyn Kitchen used to hail Mike Procter each day with 'Morning, Proccy'. To whistle a vicious bouncer past the beaks of these callow opponents, and then to smile.

Ah yes, it must be fun. To steam in like Hall, chain swinging to and fro, to cruise in like Holding, so light on your toes that umpires cannot hear you. To terrify the timid like Trueman, to force 'em to duck and weave as did Tyson. What a life! You field at long leg and lope around the boundary at your ease, no-one daring to suggest you hurry up a bit. If you bowl, helmets are donned, ambulances ordered. When Andy Roberts first played for Hampshire, his mate, Viv Richards, used to tease us with 'And here is the news. Another ambulance sent for at Southampton.'

And as soon as the other team are dismissed you sink into an armchair and sit smoking a pipe. After the game you down a few pints and chat to the opposing fast bowler, who you don't think is quite as sharp as you are. Nor dare anyone ask you to pad up to be night-watchman; you are much too fierce and temperamental. If you do bat, you hazard a wild, glorious slog, hitting the ball as high and as hard as you can, not caring if you lose your timbers.

What a life! Well, I did have my day as a fast bowler. I still have the press cuttings. The *Hong Kong Times*, carrying the story just under the news of the Iraqui troops storming through Iran, reported that 'Roebuck bowled fast and short, causing considerable discomfort.' Apparently my figures were 13–4–25–3. As ever, dry statistics fail to reflect the colour of the day, as the *Times* carried on, 'Two batsmen left the field with injuries after being struck by rising deliveries from Roebuck.' Well, there you are, see. Alas, a grave danger persists that this game might be lost to posterity. And since you badger me for the details I must, with due modesty and profound reluctance, bow to the overwhelming demand to describe the match.

You'll not be interested in our tepid innings. We, by the way, were the Mendip Acorns on tour in Malaysia, Singapore and Hong Kong. We were an improbable concoction of old, young, able and golfer. We had already played Hong Kong Cricket Club on its magnificent postage stamp ground in the hills beyond the city. We had come second in that game. This time we were facing Kowloon in the very heart of that crowded, teeming city. We scored 150 or thereabouts. Nearby pools and cocktails had proved much too attractive for long innings on that scorching day. Young Dermot Reeve, Kowloon's fast bowler, had flashed several bouncers past astonished nostrils. Our attack, alas (and alack), consisted of Mervyn Kitchen (a willing but ageing and rotund medium-pacer) and the wicket-keeper. At slip it did seem that the world was a shabby, unfair place in which to live. Where were our strapping quicks, used to carrying sheep under each arm or, if not actually eating coal, certainly cutting it, pick-axe in hand?

And then, as Jekyll turned into Hyde, so I became Fred Trueman, snorting and hissing. I growled to Kitchen (who was changing too, pink with sun, white with effort and wet with sweat) that I wanted the ball. I marked my run. Eleven paces, enough for Typhoon Tyson, enough for Holding on his short run. And quite enough for me after the previous night's activities. My first over was a range-finder, as Lieutenant Leslie Phillips' first navigational instruction in the *Navy Lark* (invariably a carefully weighed up 'left hand down a bit!') was an experiment not to be taken too literally. I was disconcerted to discover that the ball was swinging. I have enough trouble getting the ruddy thing straight as it is, without it veering off course when it is heading for the stumps. So this discovery, pleasing most bowlers, disturbed me.

As heat mounted, within and without, I strove for full pace. The broken down Ford Pop. purred as smoothly as a Renault. I let fly, hurling the ball down, flashing the ball past startled batsmen to our ageing reserve 'keeper, who hurled himself hither and thither like a jack in the box.

Kowloon's batsmen were soon battered and bruised. I scarcely bowled a short ball (that's my story, and I'm sticking to it). They kept climbing steeply off a length, like Harrier jump-jets. I slipped one through an opener, to bring to the crease a not especially heroic Pakistani. He decided to swipe every half-volley, and to dive for cover every other ball. This caused a measure of merriment for a while, though no self-respecting hairy quick could tolerate this nonsense for long. So I lengthened my run, hurled down a ball with every ounce of strength I had, and Genghis Khan returned to the sanctuary of the pavilion. Another Pakistani entered the fray, a far more robust character. He defended sternly for a few overs before essaying an ambitious hook which landed on his stumps via his aggrieved chin. He smiled the smile of defeat, raised his cap and, with a 'good afternoon', left the field in regal dignity.

Next an Aussie strode to the crease, a tough little nugget well used to fiery games of cricket. He hooked his first ball for two, laughing scornfully as he passed me, as if to say, 'Is that as fast as you can bowl?' I felt insulted, like Wes Hall seeing Brian Close advance down the pitch, undaunted by fear. I'd nail the son of doubtful parentage. Alas, the Aussie fought hard and survived until tea, limbs and wickets intact. The energy-sapping heat had taken its toll. I climbed the stairs to tea wearily, braving the barrackers who disapproved of the tearaway, blood-and-thunder fast bowler.

I tore off my damp shirt, revealing a Herculean chest, and hung it (the shirt) over the railings to dry. I strolled imperiously to tea, aware of accusing stares. Hell, this is fun. No wonder Dennis Lillee doesn't retire. After a cuppa I washed and combed my hair. I unbuttoned my fresh shirt as far as possible. Norman Teer bowled a few lobs as I rested magnificently at deep square leg. The score mounted and I watched as we slid inexorably to defeat, waiting for the final call to arms. Mervyn asked me for a last-ditch effort. Only 15 needed. I struck once, before Teer sailed over the boundary to end the game. I could not quite regain that surge of power, though.

I left the field as Popeye leaves the scenes of his carnage. I left as a fast bowler who had given his all, a man who had done a man's job. I congratulated the gritty Australian and generously enquired after the well-being of the injured, before showering and heading for the bar for a well-earned pint.

Oh well, it's back to feeble off-spinners and careworn batting these days. It was fun to be the extrovert man of action for an afternoon. No-one looks twice as I potter into tea these days, no-one polishes their helmet when I mark out my run. Oh well.

23

A Team Talk

Suddenly there is a flash of lightning and tremors slide down everyone's backbone. Our leader arises to speak to his assembled crew. A hush rolls around the room, for our captain is a formidable man. Heads hang low for fear of meeting him eye to eye. Like a Gestapo interrogator, his eye strips you naked, revealing all. Moments of horror creep back to mind. That time I had an appalling slog just after the leader had ordered me to 'get your head down, lad, and keep it down'. It all comes back. Does his roving, bloodshot eye see it?

He stands on the table now, arms aloft like the start of a Columbia film. He pauses, though he has not yet begun. The hush deepens into gloom. They say that evangelical preachers in the South create unfathomable pitches of silence before the haranguing begins. Our leader glares around him, slowly rolling his eyes. Foam seeps from the corner of his mouth. He sees into the darkest reaches, not a nook nor a cranny escapes. Shiftless souls who seek solitary seats emerge from the shadows to face the storm.

How will he begin, we wonder? No, not 'Friends, team, countrymen!' We had that last week. Nor 'Awake, arise or be for ever fall'n.' That would be too much, even for him. After all, it's only the lunch interval and they are 68 for 4. Maybe he'll sing 'Stand up and fight, men, fight for your lives.' Surely not – more likely 'Examine yourselves, examine your consciences, examine your performances.' That has a chance, a good Churchillian ring to it, and he hasn't used it for a day or two.

How does he view the morning's play, I wonder? His upper lip is curling, obviously he is not happy. Before the game he announced that the wicket 'is a line and length wicket', that 'we've got to bowl straight', that 'each of you must face your responsibilities', that 'you must keep your eye on me in the field', that 'if we can get the first five

112

out we're through the beggars', that 'this is the most important game in the club's history' and that 'you've got to be mean'. After this, the boot-stamping, the Taunton war-dance and then onto the field.

I did my best. I mean to say, it would have been a helluva catch. I was alert, fit, keen as mustard. So I dropped the ruddy thing. So what? No-one's perfect. I'd like to have seen him catch it. He'd say he'd have caught it 'between the cheeks of his backside'. He probably would have done, too.

And as for that one that slipped through my legs, well I had no chance with that. No chance at all. Bad bounce, rough outfield, spinning ball, fierce hit, no chance. So why did he pucker his eyelids as he swept past me around the room? What about Vic's effort the other day? I mean, it's not for me to criticise, I don't suppose, but it was a pretty tame effort; he could easily have caught it if he'd moved, if he was not so dozy first thing in the morning. Has he forgotten about that? I doubt it: for heaven's sake, he still remembers the four over-throws I gave away five years ago. Five years ago! We all make mistakes, these things are unavoidable, aren't they? We're only human, so you've got to be tolerant.

Oh dear. Our leader is not looking terribly tolerant. He's never thought much of namby-pamby, lily-livered liberals. He's glaring at Bill. What's Bill done? Oh hell, yes, now that really was a cock-up. He should have been backing up, he should have stopped the shy at the stumps. Yes, that was pretty poor, I'm bound to admit. He's got every right to bring that one up. Poor old Bill, he'll be on the lino (we can't afford carpet) in a minute.

He's opening his lips! My goodness, here we go, over the top, lads, all aboard. I bet he speaks well. Not as well as at Chelmsford maybe. That really was a speech. Lloyd George, Hamlet, Oscar Wilde, none of 'em could have matched it. Dame Edith Evans perhaps, but then she was a lady and they have an advantage: just look at Boadicea and Joan of Arc if you doubt it. Chelmsford was a peak. He spoke in an old-fashioned way, varying his voice from boom to hiss, throwing his metaphors into the far recesses of the dingy changing room. What was it he said? 'Now we are engaged in a great battle, testing whether this county can long endure. We meet on the great battlefield of Chelmsford. The world will little note, nor long remember what we do here. It is rather for us to be dedicated to the great task before us, that we here highly resolve that ex-Somerset players shall not have played in vain.' That's what I call a team talk! No-one knew what on earth he was on about, of course, but it felt impressive; it felt like he meant it (as Mr Macmillan said when Khrushchev ranted and raved, banging his fists on the table and shouting, 'I've got no idea what he's saying, but he seems to mean it!').

Is that steam coming out of his ears? Certainly his nostrils are twitching and his neck is reddening. I suppose captains need a bit of fire. Jeeves couldn't inspire a team, nor could Hamlet. Too much low-key wisdom on the one hand, too much dithering on the other. It's no use some nice chap saying, 'Right, chaps, we're in a bit of a pickle. The oppo are on top, lads, so let's try jolly hard.' Or even worse, 'Well, chaps, it's a nice day. Things aren't going too well, so let's at least enjoy the sun, the trees and the twittering birds.' No, that sort of stuff doesn't work – too weak-kneed. Our leader's right, really. You feel like those devils in *Paradise Lost* after our leader has spoken:

> 'They heard and were abash't, and up they sprang
> Upon the wing as men wont to watch
> On duty, sleeping, found by whom they dread
> Raise and bestir themselves ere well awake.
> Nor did they not perceive the evil plight
> In which they were, or the fire's powers not feel.'

That's the idea. Good *Land of Hope and Glory* stuff, still ringing in your ears as you take the field with confident step.

The pause is over, his throat is moving. He speaks, yes, he speaks. 'Umpires in the middle,' yells our twelfth man, with the timing of a Groucho Marx. Our leader appears angry, as an actor might if the theatre catches fire just as he is launching into his first 'To be or not to be'. Now we'll never hear that speech. Or maybe we will. At teatime.

24

Keppler Wessels

Cricket revels in men of all shapes and sizes, from Garner to Gavaskar, from Milburn to the lean Holding. It attracts men of widely different temperaments, too: the extrovert, the mean, the meek, the aggressive, the introspective. As a team game, though with a strong streak of individuality, it requires a measure of affability from even its most introvert, intense participants. Everyone must from time to time bow to the needs of the team, whether it be by taking risks or visiting the sponsor's tent.

Some men find this requirement particularly hard to fulfil. Keppler Wessels is one such. He leads a remote life, even as a cricketer. At the crease he removes himself utterly from the distractions of conversation, weather, the wife's chill and any other triviality liable to disturb him. He is absorbed, dedicated to the remorseless production of runs as if in a monastery determinedly removed from the corruption of the world. This absorption entails a tremendous mental commitment, an irrevocable refusal to tolerate lapses of concentration or mistakes caused by feeble-mindedness. Small wonder that Keppler bats on a tightrope of tension, desperate to score runs. Small wonder that he is for ever changing his technique, in a never-ending ambition to reduce the element of risk as much as humanly possible.

They said of the late and much lamented Ken Barrington that his success was founded upon a deep terror of failure, a hatred of dismissal. This may be the quality that transforms not unusually talented cricketers like Barrington and Wessels into top-class batsmen.

Reactions to dismissal vary from cricketer to cricketer. Vic Marks mutters to himself, 'Cor, bugger, I'm out.' Some shrug, others develop excuses. Some hurl their bats in a fury, others retire into their shells for a traumatic period of self-examination. Wessels, not a wild and woolly playmate in the first place, belongs to the last category. If he fails he becomes yet more inaccessible. He unstraps his pads immediately and seeks refuge in his car, in which he sits alone or with his tolerant and sympathetic wife. His colleagues might not see him again until they take the field. If failures heap upon each other, as they are wont to do in this cruel game, Wessels will sink into terrible depths, as wretched and miserable as Lear on the heath, though a good deal quieter. He will be convinced that he can never again reach 10. Team-mates do their best to restore shattered confidence, referring to his qualities and his achievements, but the depression holds until success returns.

Yet even when Wessels is in a rich vein of runs he does not sparkle with joie de vivre. No matter how many runs he scores, his appetite is not satiated. He may have hit a faultless 160 but he will still return to the pavilion at the day's end, slip into a tracksuit and be gone before most players have removed their boots. This singular approach ensures that close colleagues scarcely know Wessels any better in September than in April. Many flounder, wondering why he plays a game that brings so much anguish and so few rewards. Why play cricket, if it is not for friendship and if he is so tormented by failure? And, his colleagues ponder, how does he develop a technique sufficiently impregnable to be tolerated by that searching, unsatisfied mind?

Certainly Wessels does not need to score runs for want of any other way of life. He is intelligent, well educated and financially secure. Brought up by gregarious Dutch South Africans, his talents range far beyond cricket; he could very well have made his fortune as an international tennis player. Life might have been much easier in a world far removed from the stringent psychological demands of top-class cricket.

So why play cricket? His formative years must have imbued him with an unquenchable love of the game, not a love that expresses itself in every moment of every day, rather a burning appetite nurtured in his youth as he watched his heroes bat. He is driven by forces within to succeed at cricket, to make himself into the best, or as near the best as he possibly can. After all, as Gene Tunney said, 'A great deal has been written by experts about "natural" and "made" fighters. The boxer, like a plumber or carpenter, must learn the mechanics of his game.

The mechanics must be taught. They are never a natural inheritance.'

As a youngster, Wessels and his father persistently examined and re-examined every detail of every dismissal. They'd iron out faults with endless practice in the garden. Cosy explanations such as 'It was a good 'un' or 'Someone moved behind the bowler's arm' did not suffice. Why had he failed? How? The rigorous attitude ensured an early refusal to tolerate failure. He, a talented human being, had decided to play cricket. Therefore he must make himself very good at it. He must eradicate anything that made runs more difficult to acquire. Otherwise the whole thing would be so unsatisfactory, it would be such a waste. He must expect the highest standards, he must pile run upon run. Or else what a wilful waste of talent it would all be.

A tough approach, to the game and to himself. Other men concentrate very hard, try with all their might. None matches the discipline of Wessels' mind. Not even those other master-craftsmen, Boycott and Gavaskar, are prepared to put themselves into such an emotional coil. Gavaskar is relaxed in the dressing room, actively involved in things, as Indian cricket officials could testify. Boycott has various nicknames and anyone who dismisses him in the nets teases him mercilessly, knowing how he hates to be defeated – especially if the bowler is David Bairstow. But Wessels never appears to relax. While Mozart played billiards, Shakespeare chatted up the Dark Lady and Henry VIII married, Wessels appears to do nothing except remain in a contained relationship with his wife: a concentration on one strand of life that would terrify other men.

Keppler eschews flamboyance. In the nets, while others attempt to hit high and handsome, giving vent to frustrated dreams, Wessels blocks every ball. Every single ball. He wants to build up concentration and eliminate soft-headedness, though he is about as soft-headed as Judge Jeffreys.

Technically, Wessels is never still. He changes his stance, his grip, even his back-lift season by season, almost week by week as he strives to achieve impregnability. At the crease, however ugly or unusual his appearance, he has a reassuringly permanent air. He shuffles about 'into line, particularly early in his innings, preferring not to commit himself too early to either front or back foot. Against the new ball he presents a very straight, very dead bat. He blocks almost every ball he faces, and continues to do so as his innings unfolds. He scorns

117

elegant but unproductive strokes, whether drives to mid-off or cuts past point. Most of his early runs are scored, not in the 'V' but behind square leg or past gulley off reluctant, careworn tucks of one kind or another.

As nerves vanish Keppler gradually widens his range of strokes. His tucks merge into drives through mid-wicket and cover. He finds gaps with astonishing ease, lining up selected areas to penetrate as he solemnly defends dangerous deliveries. He accumulates runs rather like Edrich did, without anyone noticing, grasping each run as a miser grasps shillings. Most of Wessels' runs come from careful cuts, sweeps and clips. Full-blooded drives are few and far between. He prefers to persuade the ball into a space. His sweep contains a measure of risk, and is only essayed if there is no backward square leg. Wessels never hooks, preferring to bide his time until the bowlers tire and runs are more readily available.

And, like so many great players, Wessels is a masterful player of spin-bowling. He is scarcely ever out to it. Like other South Africans, Procter, Kirsten and Lamb, Wessels coolly murders spinners. With Keppler, though, it is a slow, calculated murder. He does not hit straight sixes or step away to late-cut off middle stump. He simply feeds, as ants feed on carcasses. He judges the line of the ball with great care and attacks deliveries not threatening his wicket. If he uses his feet, it is to drive along the ground. Wessels has little use for the air.

If he is on song Wessels is inevitably a formidable batsman. His every move is assessed in terms of probability. But he is also a highly skilled craftsman who knows his own capabilities. Facing Underwood on a turner in a run chase, he shuffled down to his partner to inform him, 'I'll take care of Underwood, you just stay in.' No doubt his partner was delighted, a definite improvement on the usual 'For heaven's sake, man, score some runs' or 'You fancy taking the quickie?' 'Conference' is a somewhat optimistic euphemism for most meetings between overs, in my experience!

So the inexorable grind continues. Wessels does not relent until his score passes 120. Usually. Apparently that is enough to loosen the rein a couple of notches. Even Glenn Turner only sets his sights on 40 and most of us think it would be rather nice to reach 20! With Wessels it must be at least 120.

A singular, self-contained man. His team-mates at Queensland or Hove scarcely know him any better than their rivals. When Sussex were forced to choose between Wessels and Javed Miandad several players felt Javed to be the more worthwhile colleague. Javed is a dashing, dazzling strokeplayer, a man capable of turning matches. Wessels, with his blue eyes and set jaw hidden behind helmet and visor, is the ruthless accumulator, the man to establish solid foundations.

Not much in it between Javed and Keppler. Contrasting the two is a bit like contrasting Borg and McEnroe. In those epic finals at Wimbledon in 1980 and 1981, one suspects that Wessels admired Borg's unruffled determination and clear mind, and perhaps Miandad supported the able and explosive McEnroe. Incidentally, Somerset's players were rooting for McEnroe in the 1980 final. You see, we were playing the West Indies. They had batted most of the day and were thinking of giving us 40 minutes against their pace attack. But the bowlers wanted to watch the end of that extraordinary match. So we urged McEnroe on, hoping he could last long enough for us to avoid a torrid spell with the bat.

Wessels would not have sympathised with such thoughts. He spends most of his time in the field calculating when he could expect to take guard. Fielding is a necessary evil, something to be tolerated in a life devoted to scoring runs. A harsh life.

25

Somerset v. Kent

1979 Gillette Cup Quarter-Final

Hunger for success had reached desperation at Taunton. Somerset had been dismissed from the Benson and Hedges competition by the outrage of rival clubs, amidst dark rumours and controversy. Essex, the only other team previously without honours, had seized their chance to win the B & H Cup and were streets ahead in the Championship. Their supporters were displaying banners proclaiming 'Essex 2, Somerset 0'. We wanted to win this game very, very badly.

For years Somerset had suffered at the hands of a formidable Kent team, which had included Luckhurst, Denness, Underwood, Shepherd, Asif, Knott and Woolmer at their peaks. That team had steam-rollered to success during the 1970s, often sweeping Somerset aside. Nor was there any love lost between the country cousins and the sophisticates from the South-East.

But Kent had gone a shade over the hill, as Somerset had advanced. Luckhurst and Denness were gone, Underwood, Shepherd and Asif were not quite the threats they had been. True, Tavaré, Downton and Dilley were developing, but a feeling prevailed that at last Kent's hops were ripe for picking. And meanwhile Somerset had become the most feared team in the country. Richards, Botham, Garner and Rose thriving, Marks, Roebuck and Dredge improving and Burgess, Taylor and Denning to guide the young 'uns through hard times. If Kent were not defeated by this team, we'd never beat 'em.

These various circumstances bred an atmosphere of extraordinary drama and tension. This would not be a gentle contest.

Brian Rose won the toss and decided to bat on a cloudy morning. The pitch was good, though it offered a little help to seamers while the cloud cover remained. Opening the innings, Rose defied the tight edge to the game by driving three thunderous boundaries. He'd reacted similarly in the 1978 Gillette Cup final, striking Imran for 14 in the first over, only to be dismissed shortly after. He did not survive long this time either, beaten by a fine Dilley cutter. Neither Slocombe nor I lasted, both pushing tentatively at the swinging ball. 33 for 3.

Denning, a gritty fighter and an adaptable batsman, returned to the depressing pavilion at 45. He scores heavily from his cut through point, terrifying visiting gulleys as he stands, bat ominously facing them. He can chop good balls through gulley. This time he went for the slash, Woolmer drifted one into him, cramping him, and he could only nibble it to Tavaré at slip. Downton and Tavaré caught seven catches in this innings; they were one of the most distinguished 'keeper/slip partnerships around.

Richards had batted through these failures with skill and care. Botham joined him. Usually Rose preferred to separate these powerful men: no general places his most lethal battalions next to each other. He tries to arrange his line-up by balancing men of different styles. If front-foot and back-foot players, or leg-side and off-side batsmen, or scurriers and hitters, are in together, it might unsettle the rhythm of the bowlers. This time circumstances threw Botham and Richards together. They reacted to the tension by full-blooded aggression. Botham heaved Shepherd for a towering six, and Richards advanced magnificently down the pitch to drive Underwood. If these two fired together life would not be dull!

They added 50 in nine overs, to take Somerset to 95 for 4. Then Botham glided Woolmer off his toes to Underwood at square leg. Almost immediately Richards edged Woolmer to Downton, amidst celebrations. To add to the crestfallen atmosphere, Breakwell, on the stroke of lunch, drove airily at Woolmer and Tavaré threw up the catch. Somerset slithered to the interval at 112 for 7.

The dressing room was deeply despondent, our performance had been dreadful. Only Richards roamed around the room, demanding that everyone lift up their heads, angry that hope had been abandoned. At one stage he stormed off to a nearby caravan, furious at his colleagues' downcast appearance. A formidable man, Viv.

After lunch we slid deeper into trouble as Taylor nicked Shepherd to Downton. 126 for 8. Only Garner and Jennings were left to keep

Burgess company. 'Budgie' Burgess was in his final season; he was to hang up his boots, quite literally, a month later at Trent Bridge. In his career he had often approached achievements worthy of his astonishing ball-playing ability, only to fall inexplicably short and to continue his role as a useful county cricketer. He could beat any of his talented colleagues at any ball game. He used to sit in a chair to play tabletennis (itself an insight into his abilities and failings!) and still hammered all comers. Yet something within him prevented fulfilment, some demon that drove him to seek perfection rather than giving rein to his ability to produce the spectacular hitting of which he was capable.

Of his partners, Garner often informed doubting mates that he could bat. He explained how he could 'flick' the ball here, 'lick' it there and 'lash' it yonder, though Viv Richards' eyes told a different story. As for Jennings, well he went in below Garner!

'Big Bird' held on as Burgess gathered runs. So many times Budgie had taken the soft option to blaze his way out of trouble. This time he worked at his game, as if recognising that if we lost this day he'd never know success in his career. This was his last chance.

Urged on by the crowd, Burgess developed his innings, batting with a high degree of skill. Garner decided to cut loose. He whipped Asif off middle stump over square leg, to our glee and Asif's consternation. Next ball he tried to repeat the dose and lost his leg stump. Burgess looked to the heavens, and Garner slammed his bat into the turf as he made a forlorn trail towards the pavilion.

Jennings, scarcely a batsman at all, joined Burgess and he, too, chose this day to hang on. With Burgess he added 33 valuable runs and, far more importantly, lifted Somerset's spirits. After all, 190 exceeded even Viv's lunchtime predictions. The recovery inspired the team, restored the faith of the taut crowd. In the 1978 Gillette Cup final we had scored over 200, yet had taken the field despondent at having barely played an attacking shot in the last few overs, for obscure reasons.

One more advantage of our innings: Garner was still in a very dark mood. Aggrieved at his dismissal, he retired into his shell, building up determination to bowl with pace like fire. Kent had a reputation for being ill at ease against pace, often losing to Middlesex who boasted the formidable Wayne Daniel. Garner could be as nasty as anyone if his mellow mind was sufficiently motivated. If he bowled at absolutely full pace, Kent might have an interesting afternoon.

In his first over, Garner sprinted to the crease, not running on water as he sometimes appears to do. He searched for rhythm and thrust. He bowled three no-balls, but reared one up to Johnson who fended it gently to Burgess in the gulley. Burgess, not yet recovered from his innings, promptly dropped the chance amidst groans. A hero one minute, a villain the next!

Botham bowled as fast as he could, but conceded yards to Garner who roared in, an intimidating sight, hurling down the ball at an awesome pace. Suddenly Garner yorked Johnson, bringing a massive, sustained roar of relief. Tavaré was next in. He appeared nervous, white as a sheet. He jumped into a fiery delivery, it brushed his glove and Taylor snapped up the chance. Another shattering shout, and Richards and Botham rushed over to applaud Garner. Kent were shaken to their very foundations.

Asif joined Woolmer, Kent's most experienced and talented players. Woolmer seemed as unruffled as ever, as if he had adopted Cowdrey's dignified and unhurried style. He pushed at Garner, edging the ball between first and second slip. Richards moved across for it but Botham stuck out a meaty left hand in an instant and hung on to a staggering catch. He hurled the ball to the heavens. No-one else could have taken such an astonishing, instinctive catch. Except perhaps Richards.

Kent captain Alan Ealham flashed hugely at his first two balls, evidently determined to present a bold front. It appeared to us that Kent were out of control, a ship with a broken rudder. Ealham's third ball smashed through a meek defence to uproot the middle stump, and a veritable explosion of noise erupted. Kent 19 for 4. Defeat had turned into at least a hint of victory in two dramatic overs.

Shepherd came in to partner Asif. Two flamboyant strokeplayers. Garner needed a rest but Botham persevered, giving every ounce of his immense strength. He'd bowled without luck, clutching his hair as his outswinger slid past the bat time and again. Kent crept to 40 for 4, and we had been 45 for 4. Had they survived the worst of the storm?

Asif began to assert himself, hooking Botham to the boundary. A wicket was needed lest our momentum be lost. Asif flashed at a wide half-volley, a rare bad ball. He failed to move his feet, and edged the shot onto his wicket as Botham saluted a triumph at last. Asif hung his head and Richards hurtled to Botham, smacking their hands together West Indian style. 40 for 5.

Still Kent persevered, as Jennings and Burgess trundled away. Shepherd swung lustily at Jennings, skying the ball towards long stop. Botham at slip immediately charged after it, for all the world like an All Black no. 8 going for the line. He caught the ball, hands out-stretched, at full throttle: another extraordinary catch, remarkable athleticism from a man who had bowled eight fast overs with the new ball.

Only the youngsters were left to chase the rainbow. Cowdrey drove across Burgess, skying a tantalising chance to Breakwell at mid-off. Dennis, a jumpy character at the best of times, hovered under the catch. Rose did not watch the ball descend, turning his back as he saw who was circling uneasily beneath it. But Breakwell hung on, white as a sheet. 59 for 7 at tea. A relieved ovation sent Somerset to a happy dressing room. If ever a game had been conclusively turned in an hour, this one had been in that explosive opening burst.

The rest was straightforward; the mopping-up operations did not take long. Garner ended with 5 for 11, Botham with 3 for 15. A stunning match. Most memorable for Garner's fierce onslaught, Botham's brilliant catches and the frenzied noise of a partisan crowd. They were heights that cannot be scaled every day.

SOMERSET

B. C. Rose	c Downton b Dilley	15
P. A. Slocombe	c Tavaré b Dilley	2
I. V. A. Richards	c Downton b Woolmer	44
P. M. Roebuck	c Downton b Jarvis	6
P. W. Denning	c Tavaré b Woolmer	3
I. T. Botham	c Underwood b Woolmer	29
G. I. Burgess	not out	50
D. Breakwell	c Tavaré b Woolmer	8
D. J. S. Taylor	c Downton b Shepherd	2
J. Garner	b Asif	12
K. F. Jennings	b Shepherd	7
Extras		12
		—
Total (59.2 overs)		190

Fall of wickets: 1–16, 2–21, 3–33, 4–45, 5–95, 6–102, 7–110, 8–126, 9–157.

Bowling: Jarvis 11–1–40–1; Dilley 12–3–28–2; Woolmer 12–2–28–4; Shepherd 10.2–2–41–2; Underwood 9–4–26–0; Asif 5–0–15–1.

	KENT	
R. A. Woolmer	c Botham b Garner	6
G. W. Johnson	b Garner	1
C. J. Tavaré	c Taylor b Garner	0
Asif Iqbal	b Botham	10
A. G. E. Ealham	b Garner	0
J. N. Shepherd	c Botham b Jennings	9
C. S. Cowdrey	c Breakwell b Burgess	12
P. R. Downton	b Garner	6
G. R. Dilley	lbw Botham	0
D. L. Underwood	c Taylor b Botham	0
K. B. S. Jarvis	not out	0
Extras		16
Total (28.4 overs)		60

Fall of wickets: 1–14, 2–14, 3–17, 4–19, 5–40, 6–54, 7–59, 8–60, 9–60.

Bowling: Garner 9.4–2–11–5; Botham 10–4–15–3; Burgess 5–3–12–1; Jennings 4–2–6–1.

Somerset won by 130 runs.

26

Jewel Of The East

Forewarned is forearmed, as the sages have it. So visitors to Somerset are kindly introduced to the horrors of scrumpy. Sometimes, though, it is more fun to let the unsuspecting guest slip on the rural banana-skin. Soon after he arrived from Barbados, Hallam Moseley approached a host of green stinging nettles at speed in pursuit of a cricket ball. If any kind soul thought to warn him as to the hazards of his course, he held his peace. The effect was spectacular, akin to Fred Astaire with St Vitus' Dance. As a new recruit to the cider-county, Sunil Gavaskar avoided nettles, scrumpy, the Wurzels and skittles with the ease born of experience. Eating curry and sleeping on beds of nails encourages a healthy suspicion of the strange habits of the Occident.

Mind you, Sunil did make one slight mistake. Out of the kindness of his heart he fed a poor, stray, lonely pigeon that appeared on his window sill. Alas, wisdom and generosity oft suggest different paths. The pigeon knew when he (or she) was on to a good thing. 'Free grub at the Gavaskars,' he called to his mates who arrived with manic optimism, chirping at the window like a barber-shop quartet in the Depression. Sunny's flat began to resemble Nelson's column. One wondered whether the SAS would need to be called in. Or if things got really bad, would Botham turn up with his air-gun?

Sunny arrived at Taunton with the aura of the great batsman. Everyone was a little nervous. But after the pigeon incident (sounds like one of the 'Causes of the First World War'), Somerset players realised that Gavaskar had a touch of Harry Worth and need not be taken too seriously. Apparently simple operations were beyond him. He was never quite able to release the hand-brake on his car. It was Hyde Park Corner in the rush hour when he remembered he had left his wallet at The Oval. He was appalled at the thought of driving in

London. And neither he nor his wife had the slightest notion of how to cook and wash without their retinue of servants.

Oh yes, and Sunny is terrified of dogs. Petrified, in fact. If one appears on the field during a Gavaskar innings his composure is shattered. Needless to say, Ian Botham missed no opportunity to invite dogs into our dressing room; or if he couldn't find a dog, Ian would offer a few hidden woofs of his own. In either case Sunil beat a faster retreat than any Italian army yet recorded.

These vagaries ensured that Sunny merged easily into the Somerset team. Suspicions of Oriental mysticism raised by Derek Taylor (who says he once played for Leyton Orient) vanished. Someone who is defeated by a hand-brake does not for long remain on a pedestal: the gloves came off, and Sunil was teased and cajoled with the rest. His nickname was 'Swoop', a loose description of his fielding at mid-on. Where most fieldsmen hurry towards the ball in order to intercept it more easily, Swoop ambles along, leaving it until the last possible moment to dart out a hand to effect the stop. Naturally this produces tremendous applause from the crowd, accompanied by an outrageously innocent smile from Gavaskar. In the field Sunny did retain a little of the majesty of the Raj, though. He never dived. Apparently it is dangerous to dive in India, for fear of the tetanus injections that follow. And Swoop was too old a dog to learn new tricks, or so he said.

Sunil Gavaskar is well able to cope with the company of other cricketers. Though he does not smoke, drink or swear (Botham says he once exclaimed, 'Oh, my goodness', but Botham's been watching *It Ain't 'Arf 'Ot, Mum* too often), Swoop soon captures the atmosphere of a dressing room and thrives in it. For, in a mellow, gentle way, Gavaskar gives as good as he gets. It did not take him long to remark upon the stark resemblance between the Taunton dressing room and the Black Hole of Calcutta. More often his humour is the humour of understatement. After several severe maulings he suggested that 'our bowling seems more friendly than theirs'. And with Ian Botham on 198 one teatime he produced a calculator and informed Ian that he was on course for 418 not out – more if he accelerated once his eye was in!

No doubt had 'Swoop' served in the court of Henry VIII he would not have ranted and raved about the iniquities of the Pope. He would have slipped up to Henry and speculated as to whether Popes weren't getting a bit big for their mitres nowadays. The seeds sown, he would then have withdrawn. This quiet underplaying of personality may be an Indian trait, a product of a humble philosophy. Certainly Sunil is a remarkably balanced individual. He does hold some extraordinary views, though. He regards cricket as 'only a game', defeat as 'not the end of the world'. He even has a regular job. Nor is he especially impressed by his own achievements, regarding success and failure as the playthings of the fates. Were he English, of course, one would assume he had had an unfortunate accident as a youth. Cricket only a game? There are limits to man's credulity.

Sunil brought his family with him to Somerset. Not many international cricketers take their parents, wife and son with them on their travels. Some travel specifically to escape from their entourage! But the Gavaskars enjoyed Taunton immensely. Little Rohan (6), whose hero is Viv Richards, fairly revelled in playing with the children of Swoop's colleagues. He joined in fielding practices with gusto, batted left-handed (preferably with a Jumbo – Viv uses one) and popped into the dressing room when he was lonely, braving even the dark threats of fierce Uncle Ian to seek Papa's solace.

Maybe it is not surprising that the Family Gavaskar came to Somerset. Taunton must have been an oasis of calm after the strain of life in Bombay. Sunil receives 85 fan letters a day at home (Rohan gets 5!). He dare not venture into the streets for fear of being mobbed by admirers. A Sunday League game, the most exacting cricket he played in his season with us, must have been like a hit in the park after India v. Pakistan at Madras. Small wonder that Sunil relished a few months of relaxed cricket as part of a modest county team playing in a mild provincial town.

Meeting this gentle man, it is easy to forget his marvellous Test record. That ready smile must conceal nerves of steel, for Gavaskar has scored well-nigh 6000 Test runs, including 23 centuries. He has formed the backbone of Indian batting for a decade. This in a country where cricket is followed with fanatical zeal, where success can bring the hazards of worship and failure the pain of ignominy.

No wonder that he is happier when someone else is carrying the burdens of leadership. He has enough curry on his plate already. Much more relaxing to be an ordinary member of the team, able to release tension once the day's deeds are done. And no wonder that Swoop is a little impractical. The atmosphere of calm chaos that pervades his life must help restore his powers. As the fates blow in the wind it is fortunate that Gavaskar has that self-deprecating humour, too. If he took things to heart for too long his burden might seem profoundly heavy.

In any event, for all his foibles in everyday life, as a batsman Gavaskar is superbly professional. His method has survived the most rigorous examination. Runs have been scored against Roberts and Holding in the West Indies, Snow and Botham in England, Thomson in Australia and Underwood in India. Sunil is a craftsman, master of the techniques of his profession. As a craftsman, he continually re-examines his methods and makes minor adjustments. To improve his performance on English pitches Sunny decided to use a larger, heavier bat. This helped him to stand upright. And he played the ball a little later in England, lest he be defeated by unpredictable movement. These were the changes made to counter particular threats, the product of careful thought by a batsman who knows he must attend to the details of his science.

With a performance as excellent as his there is no doubt that Gavaskar is extraordinarily gifted. Yet defining his peculiar talent is not easy. His personality is too self-effacing for his batting to be too dramatic. Nor does Sunil adopt an idiosyncratic stroke as his hallmark (like Richards' on-drive, Boycott's square-cut and Zaheer's off-drive). He scores without fuss and at his own pace. His excellence lies in the mastery of the simple principles of batting as they have been handed down the generations. His head is always still. He watches the ball with the utmost care. If he chooses to take a risk it is calculated, not an undisciplined reaction to a tense situation.

Somerset folk enjoyed Gavaskar's visit. His batting was discussed from Charlton Adam to Farrington Gurney. Peter Robinson, our coach, was pleased, too. Until Sunny arrived, most youngsters seemed either to smash good-length balls through mid-wicket (à la Richards), or dispatch them over extra cover (à la Botham), or play and miss at them (à la modesty forbids). Discriminating between the good ball and the bad crept back into favour during the season Sunny was with us and Peter found himself sleeping a lot better!

That 1980 season also settled one long-standing argument between Vic Marks and myself. Vic, a little on the short side, argues that big men have an advantage at the crease in that their reach is so much greater. I, on the other hand, as a man of some stature, hold that the small batsman has a tremendous, almost overwhelming advantage in that it is so much easier for him to hook, cut and use his feet. Watching Gavaskar, I felt I'd won the day. Indeed, the only confusion now felt at Taunton is why our reserve wicket-keeper, Trevor Gard, a man of similar size to Sunil, cannot bat as well or hit as powerfully!

Everyone at Taunton was sad when 'Swoop' returned to Bombay. It had been fun studying him, and fun trying to detect the tough, determined core that lurks behind those humorous, fairly mischievous eyes.

27

A Benefit Game

The season is over. We've overthrown our last overthrow, dropped our last catch until April next. Autumn is with us, bringing squally showers and even colder winds. For six months we'll remember the season, its triumphs and its disappointments. We'll see the wife and the kids, follow our soccer teams and grumble about the Government and modern youth. Only a few duties remain before the final curtain falls. We must roam the length and breadth of Somerset playing friendlies for this year's beneficiary, Peter Denning.

'Dasher' Denning is well loved in Somerset. His stubborn, earthy nature disguises a pride in his county and a determination to 'do the buggers'. 'The buggers', it emerges, are the opposition. His father butchers in Chewton Mendip, and most of Peter's abrupt views and grizzly shots come straight from the shop. He chops the ball past point with gritty defiance. 'Don't get out,' he'll growl at you at the crease. 'Don't get out to these buggers.' He is not one to make a fuss if he does fall, though. If he has scored 184 or been dismissed first ball, he'll walk grumpily back to the pavilion, sit down, remove his pads and light a small cigar. No belabouring of umpires or morose head in hands for Dasher Denning. If he has scorched the earth with his short-arm drives he'll explain, 'Well, it was up there, so it had to go, didn't it?' A simple approach to batting which, accompanied by that rural twang, attracts the County folk at Taunton.

As he's played for us since 1969 he's been granted a benefit. He's arranged games in hitherto unsuspected depths of Somerset, in villages and hamlets known only to Dasher. We discover villages that rustle through the years irrespective of change of Manchester United managers, villages that regard new-fangled farming methods with the very deepest suspicion. Even those of us well used to Somerset lanes struggle to find some of these places as we traipse disconsolately from gate to church. Our West Indian contingent suffer terribly. They never quite understand why they invariably end up following a herd of cows or a combine harvester (even though they like their cereals and milk for breakfast!). Often they visit a few farms along the way, as a road fades into a lane which merges into some rustic backyard.

Nor do signposts help the weary traveller in these parts. If you don't know the way you'll get lost, signposts or no signposts. Hedges, cross-roads, tractors, sheep and ditches conspire to confuse any visitor. If you happen to observe a farmer and stop to ask him, 'Where the bloody hell is this?', his reply might not be as helpful as intended. 'Ah, see, let oi tell 'ee,' he'll say, adding, 'Thilk way down younder, zilch twassock be zuch astween . . .' Bajans and Mendipians may both speak English, but conversations tend to have somewhat prolonged pauses, as stunned brains try to unravel an extraordinary succession of sounds.

So, when Dasher (or 'Nipper', or 'Grump') Denning tells Viv, Joel and Moses (the West Indian entrant for a Eurovision Song Contest?) that they are due in Frog Marten at 2 pm, a shudder results, with a widening, a whitening of eyes following. Moses runs around saying, 'It'll be all right, mate' as Corporal Jones would bellow 'Don't panic, don't panic.' Joel, in a deep bass, sighs, 'Oh, rasta man', and Viv hunts for his mate, Peter McCombe. Not a wise move by Viv, for Peter hails from the back streets of Glasgow and spends most of his time roaring 'Stitch that', 'Och, aye', and 'Ruddy English can't play football'.

Still, usually we arrive in the end. Farmers do not worry if we are a little late, nothing ever runs to plan on a farm. Vic Marks, son of a Somerset farmer, mutters from time to time about it being too dry for the potatoes and too wet for the wheat. Too dry and too wet! Hard to please, farmers.

Only once did we arrive very late, so late that the game started without us. We drove in to discover our two guest players defending stoically in front of a confused crowd, surprised to discover the stars of *Emmerdale Farm* opening the innings for Somerset.

Somerset has a tradition of unpredictable genius, even in proper cricket. For years, supporters treasured occasional inspired triumphs which relieved the repeated heavy defeats. They enjoyed the sudden, brilliant defiance of the odds, they enjoyed the characters, the flow of scrumpy and brandy, the broken-down appearance. With Garner, Richards, Popplewell and Denning the characters remain, from the grumpy to the joyous. Nor is the cricket often humdrum; a few successes have not dented the colourful reputation. The trouble is, of course, that if supposedly serious games are so entertaining, what is left for Cheddar or Baltonsborough? You need not worry, we are not short of ideas.

Most professionals play benefit matches in a relaxed but orthodox manner. A cricketer is a cricketer for all that, and likes to show it. You cannot rely upon that with Somerset. We've never actually lost on a village green yet, but we've come mighty close, most notably at Sparkford, where Joel Garner had to change to rescue us!

Tactics vary. Viv Richards bowls nonchalant leg-spinners. Ian Botham keeps wicket, Hallam Moseley signs autographs, Dennis Breakwell hides behind a tree. Efforts are made to confuse the umpire; we casually change ends after five balls, or stand gaping at him when he calls 'over' after the sixth. Or the 'keeper holds the ball as the bowler apparently delivers it, hurling it into the air supported by raucous appeals for a catch behind the wicket. Umpires need to be well-balanced men to survive, utterly certain of their sanity, rather like the gentleman we met on a visit to a mental hospital. It was dance night, and very lively, too. This gentleman, with a daffodil sticking remarkably from one ear, crept cunningly up to us to warn us to beware the other patients as 'They're all raving lunatics!'

Probably our most intriguing performance in a benefit game was down in Exeter. Rumours reached Taunton that Exeter intended to beat us, to show professional cricket in its true light. This steeled us to keep our heads down, to sniff the ball out and to watch it onto the bat. We managed to obey cricket's complex instructions for most of the game. But once a decisive victory was certain, all hell let loose. We had lost time to make up. We lined up in the slips as a rugby threequarter line, passing the ball from 'keeper to a running first slip and so sweeping across the ground. And we stood in line from mid-on to mid-off, charging at the batsman as the bowler ran in, hunting like a pack, to see who could be the first to retrieve the ball. This caused considerable confusion, and was not universally regarded as hilarious, but after all it was our day off and we had not wanted to play a 'Test' match in the first place.

It's not usually quite as anarchic as that. Somerset players are willing autograph signers and ready drinkers, so good spirits are the rule. After all, it's fun to see Richards, Botham, Garner and Rose batting in the local field. Our benefit games attract large audiences, including hundreds of schoolboys out to see if their dad, or Mr Dodds the grocer, can dismiss the great Vivian Richards. And Mr Dodds has an excellent chance of doing just that. You can live on such things for years.

We played a benefit game in Braunton a while back, a fairly typical affair, and here is my report on it.

Somerset v. Braunton

After fruitless searches on indecipherable maps we discovered that Braunton was somewhere in North Devon. It is hidden amongst baffling lanes, tucked away from any major road. We found it, Colin Dredge ('Bert') and I. We weaved to the ground through fields, huts, fences and straw-bales. At the ground we learned that we were supposed to be back in town wining and dining at the pub, as our hosts shrewdly sought to even things up a bit. Amidst curses from the driver, which Bert bore in good stead, having played golf with him, the two of us followed our noses and lunched.

A large, patient crowd await our return and are delighted to see Botham and Richards. The aforementioned observe the short boundaries and are happy, too. After a token toss, we bat first. Our order is decided by who can find a corner to change and who cannot. Breakwell opens with Trevor Gard – not Hobbs and Sutcliffe quite, but a nice variety of chatter and silence nonetheless. I'm at three, so I retire to the gents' as play starts. Immediately a hilarious cheer erupts. I fear the worst. I peer out. Dennis Breakwell is striding back to the pavilion as pleased as Punch, his Charlie Chaplin moustache twitching. Apparently he has been caught at long-off first ball. Long-off? First ball? As Joel says, 'What happenin', man? Too much lawlessness around here.' Word has it that Dennis was on a £5 bet that he couldn't hit his first ball for six. He lost by a yard. He spends the afternoon roaming around asking, 'Where was Moses when the lights went out?' Answer, 'In the dark!'

I arrive belatedly at the crease. Trevor Gard, a man of few words and less teeth, is grinning a toothless grin. Why? First ball, I poke forward a shade winely. The ball rises slowly and I study it with interest as it climbs past my nose. A piece of turf follows shortly after. Trevor is looking even more pleased. At least I understand that Mona Lisa smile now.

I survive a while, hitting the ball and ducking the grass. Upon my dismissal, Viv enters the arena, full of majestic poise. He is almost immediately dismissed, a victim of a flyer (a 'take-off job', as we call them). It only takes one ball, from an undertaker or a window cleaner, to defeat the greatest of batsmen. Temporarily stunned, the crowd is not sure whether to cheer or cry. Ian Botham wipes out disappointment, laying about himself with immense gusto. He breaks no windows, the houses are too close! Ian is a valuable asset in benefit games, prepared to carry on in torrential rain, willing to entertain by hoofing a soccer ball about if necessary.

Eventually our innings collapses and we descend on the tea tent, ploughing into an assortment of cakes, sausages and sandwiches. This rather affects our performance thereafter.

One way or another I am appointed to keep the wickets. Not a much sought-after position. Professionals know how to make complete idiots of colleagues and they will succeed pretty well with me.

Dennis Breakwell opens the bowling, too. Ever the life and soul of things, Dennis launches what is euphemistically referred to as our attack with his impersonation of Sir Gary Sobers. Next he delivers the ball whilst looking towards extra cover, then with his eyes firmly shut. His first two balls produce edges to our startled 'keeper, who nevertheless catches both. He is thought to be the only man to have caught catches off the first two deliveries of his 'keeping career. At Braunton.

After this we decide to introduce even worse bowlers. Nothing untoward happens on the field. Someone did once end up upside-down on barbed wire as he toppled over the boundary attempting a catch. It was frightening for a moment, but a novel sight once it was obvious that his injuries were minor.

Popplewell, an infectious enthusiast, does a few handstands, otherwise Braunton collapse in relative tranquillity. No desperate struggles this time, no need to send post haste for Garner. No, everything jogs along fine and dandy. Braunton score some runs, most of 'em can boast of having hit Botham or Richards to the boundary. After that, a few beers in the tent. Then a function to attend, before returning home to put the feet up, to reflect upon the closeness of laughter and tears, and to ponder that the next game is six months away.

28

Rupert's Roses

by Nigel Popplewell

Hitherto it has been widely believed that Brian Rose is the most eminent gardener in English cricket. Not so. Since June, Peter Roebuck has developed an avid enthusiasm, a growing enthusiasm, for all things horticultural. Evidence as to his activities before June is conflicting. Peter (Rupert) remembers cutting his parents' grass in August 1973, but his mother casts doubt upon this recollection, though she does concede that he once watered the indoor plants. Alas, several of them were plastic.

Peter's plot lies deep in the wilds of West Monkton, flanked by well groomed and elegant gardens. Neighbours were confused when the name changed from a reliable 'Tamaris' to a suspicious 'Walesa', though their concern soon switched two houses down when a 6′ 8″ black man appeared with rake and brush as the new tenant of no. 16.

Rupert's back garden is about eight yards square, surrounded by flower beds and hedges, and it was in these that there appeared, in July, a number of flowers. As the garden was not a sea of colour, more of a pond, Rupert's thoughts turned towards growth and development by August. He decided to embark upon a course of pruning and sought some gardening shears. Alas, none were to be found but he was not deterred. Throughout July and August our neighbours (for I share this happy abode) watched as one of the 'eight for the 80s' attacked his azaleas with a bread-knife.

The results of his selective 'weeding' remain to be seen. His policy of pulling up anything which had no flower was not one I found recommended in any literature, but he explained the theory to me so convincingly that I am sure that, when we return next April, the flower beds will be entirely clear of such evil parasitic nasties as bind-weed, hogweed, tumbleweed and any other weeds endemic to West Monkton.

I am all for digging up the back garden to grow a few of the simpler English vegetables – asparagus, artichokes, aubergines – but Rupert is utterly disdainful of mere foodstuffs. As he potters around his garden (*his* garden), doting on his daffodils, patting successful roses on the head, he exudes a warm glow of satisfaction. It's as if he and his flowers had triumphed in horrendously appalling conditions, as if they have surived the conspiracy of weather, greenfly and vegetables – and all with one bread-knife and one frying pan!

As a gardener, his pièce de résistance is his mowing. On many a summer morning I have awoken at 7.00 am to the pleasant droning of the Flymo as he passes beneath the window. He mows with intense concentration, broken only by the occasional curse as he beheads a rose – giving the impression that you are in the company of a true craftsman. Indeed, by the end of the season he was wielding the Flymo as judiciously as his Jumbo, much to the relief of the herbaceous border. Casual passers-by refrain from hiding behind trees to watch his mowing, though the sight of Joel Garner pushing the self-same mower two doors down still attracts an audience.

Peter tends the flowers lovingly, supported by generous supplies of water from above. He possesses neither sprinkler nor watering can, preferring to dampen tender buds with rushes from milk bottle or frying pan. Kitchen utensils are used sporadically over the stove and frequently over the plants. He also decided that his flowers respond to music and many a summer's evening has ended with the sound of 'Blowin' in the Wind' as Peter serenades his favourite nasturtium.

The house is nice, too, but he hardly spends any time inside. Mostly he roams around grumbling about 'these dreadful green things that keep strangling all my plants'. Perhaps one day when he's in Leeds or London I'll get out a spade (or, I daresay, a spoon) and start my vegetable patch. Then I'll flee the country!

Glossary

by Victor Marks

A definition of some of the words used in this book.

JAFFA: The sort of delivery by which our captain is generally dismissed – an unplayable ball. In the days of the amateur it was known variously as a purler, snorter or humdinger. In fact, real Jaffas rarely take wickets because they miss everything. Ask Joel Garner.

UNPLAYABLE BALL: A term used by batsmen dismissed within a few balls of taking guard, to describe any delivery responsible for their demise. Used by bowlers to describe any ball which gets a wicket.

CAUGHT IN THE BOX: Not quite as painful as it sounds. The 'box' is a fielding position often patrolled by Graham Burgess; thus it covers a large area between short extra and short mid-wicket.

TO SEE THE BALL LIKE A FOOTBALL: As far as I am concerned this only happens in pre-season training or in the nets. Ask Viv Richards.

MINEFIELD: A dangerous wicket where the ball behaves unpredictably. Batsmen will tell you that 75 per cent of all wickets come within this category.

SHIRT-FRONT: A placid wicket where the ball refuses to deviate in any direction. Bowlers will tell you that 75 per cent of all wickets come within this category.

LBW: A mistake by the umpire.

CRICKED NECK: An affliction exclusive to spin-bowlers, especially when bowling from the pavilion end at Taunton to the likes of Mike Procter or Zaheer. It results from the sudden strain on the muscles of the neck caused by the bowler trying to follow the trajectory of the ball back over his head and onto the pavilion roof – or further.

LEG-CUTTERS: Deliveries at which batsmen play and miss outside the off stump when Richie Benaud is commentating.

ATTEMPTED YORKER: A bowler's definition for any full toss.

CAUGHT AT THE WICKET: A problem common to batsmen who have (a) indulged in a surfeit of Guinness the previous evening or (b) partaken of an especially potent vindaloo. This problem is guaranteed to beset those who have combined (a) and (b). Can always be detected when the wicket-keeper stands back to the slow left-armer.

THE CIRCUS: A very new term popularised by John le Carré. The true definition has yet to emerge, but there are numerous possibilities:

1 Benefit games
2 Joel Garner and Trevor Gard sharing a partnership
3 Team talks
4 The John Player Sunday League
5 County committees.

A SPORTING DECLARATION: Any declaration which the captain has completely misjudged and which results in defeat.

SEVEN-A-SIDE: A term used to describe any team who lose the toss and have to bat on a 'minefield' when Joel Garner is bowling.

FIVE-A-SIDE: Refers to the above team when their innings is over.

A PAIR: Happens to a batsman who receives one Jaffa in each innings of the same game, thus resulting in two noughts against his name on the score-sheet.

A KING PAIR: When Viv Richards suffers from the above.

RED INK: An affectionate term used by batsmen. Refers to the practice of using red to indicate a 'not out' in the scorebook.

GOING FOR A FEW: Not, as you may think, used to indicate a visit to the 'local', but a term used to describe a bowler's performance when bowling to the likes of Mike Procter or Zaheer.

PUT HIM DOWN: This is the fate awaiting any fielder when he returns to the dressing room having dropped a catch.

WESTON FESTIVAL: This is the date on which the monsoon usually hits the county.

NO-BALL: Term used by the umpires. Usually refers to the best ball you have bowled that game, month or season!

BUFFET BALL: A disappointing delivery, inviting the batsman to help himself to runs.

WATCHIT BALL: A poor ball; the bowler cries 'Watch it!' to warn his close fielders of imminent danger.

Also in Unwin Paperbacks

Great One-Day Cricket Matches
David Lemmon

The one-day, limited-over cricket match has been one of the most revolutionary innovations made in cricket this century. Many of them have produced breathtaking finishes.

David Lemmon's book recalls some of the most memorable occasions from World Cup finals to League matches and includes two fascinating, nostalgic accounts of one-day games played before the first limited-over competition in 1963.

For this paperback three accounts of 1983 matches have been included.

The Guide to Real Village Cricket
Robert Holles

For the cooler winter months this paperback provides a warming nostalgic glimpse of village cricket. This selection of laws and anecdotes, liberally sprinkled with Roy Raymonde's delightful cartoons, will enchant every advocate of our national game.

'One of the funniest cricket books I have ever read. The stories, all of which have more than a grain of truth, are riotous'

The Cricketer

'Marvellous value'

Daily Mail

'The illustrations are sheer delight'

Club Cricketer

A Funny Turn
Confessions of a Cricketing Clown
Ray East in association with Ralph Dellor

Illustrated by Bill Tidy

Is modern first-class cricket too serious for the players to enjoy? Ray East doesn't think so. He is blessed with an instinct for seeing the funny side of things, and his spontaneous humour has lit up grounds all over the cricketing world. Now the joker of the county circuit has provided accounts of some of the most amusing episodes from his long career both in county cricket and on tours abroad. Opponents, umpires, colleagues and captains all provide the raw material for his stories, and he is quite able to see a joke against himself.

This Curious Game of Cricket
George Mell

Illustrated by Bill Tidy

Cricket attracts freakish events. What happens for example when a hedgehog stops play. Fortunately there is one player well-equipped to deal with invading hedgehogs. Dealing with other pitch invasions can require greater ingenuity and sometimes a fair amount of courage. This book also includes reports of 'Ostrich stopped play' and an interruption by a poisonous snake. There are other diverting stories: a match where all the players were on horseback; a bowling analysis of 0–0–4–0; 286 runs off one hit and even matches which started at 4 a.m. or earlier. This collection will pass the time during the breaks for rain and delight all followers of cricket during the long winter months.

Phoenix from the Ashes

The Story of the England–Australia Series 1981

Mike Brearley

Every so often the world of sport throws up an event or performance quite out of the ordinary. Cricket has had more than its fair share. What was so unusual about the events of 1981, however, was that it provided not one match but three which caught the public's imagination – and brought Test cricket back to a popularity it had not enjoyed since the Centenary Test of 1977.

In the Third Test at Headingley, England, seemingly about to lose the Ashes, came back from the brink of defeat to win by 18 runs. At Edgbaston, barely a fortnight later, England repeated the performance, bowling out Australia for 121 in their fourth innings, to win this time by 29. In the Fifth Test the margin was greater – 103 runs – but not before Australia had threatened to win the game with something to spare. The Sixth Test was a draw, but one which contained three centuries, Lillee's best Test performance ever (7 for 89) and a nail-biting finish. But beyond the actual results there was the spectacle of the series being turned on its head by the performance of one man – Ian Botham, who had failed in the first two Tests and yet who in the Third scored a magnificent 149 not out, in the Fourth took a match-winning 5 wickets for 11 runs, and in the Fifth scored one of the great centuries of all time, 118 in 123 minutes.

There have been remarkable series and remarkable matches before, but never has an England captain so much at the heart of his team's success, or so able to express the full story of that success, written his account with such honesty and perception.

Also in Unwin Paperbacks

Cricket World Cup '83 *Derek Hodgson*	£1.95 ☐
A Funny Turn *Ray East*	£1.75 ☐
Gerald Davies: An Autobiography	£1.50 ☐
Great One-Day Cricket Matches *David Lemmon*	£1.75 ☐
The Guide to Real Village Cricket *Robert Holles*	£1.95 ☐
Phoenix from the Ashes *Mike Brearley*	£1.95 ☐
A Question of Cricket *Derek Lodge*	£1.75 ☐
This Curious Game of Cricket *George Mell*	£1.75 ☐

All these books are available at your local bookshop or newsagent, or can be ordered direct by post. Just tick the titles you want and fill in the form below.

_____

Name...

Address ....

....

....

Write to Unwin Cash Sales, PO Box 11, Falmouth, Cornwall TR10 9EN.

Please enclose remittance to the value of the cover price plus:

UK: 50p for the first book plus 20p for the second book, thereafter 14p for each additional book ordered, to a maximum charge of £1.68.

BFPO and EIRE: 50p for the first book plus 20p for the second book and 14p for the next 7 books and thereafter 8p per book.

OVERSEAS: 85p for the first book plus 23p per copy for each additional book.

Unwin Paperbacks reserve the right to show new retail prices on covers, which may differ from those previously advertised in the text or elsewhere. Postage rates are also subject to revision.